JULY 21, 2008

Paths in The Brier Patch
2nd Edition

By Dr. William Lindsey McDonald
Illustrated by Dorothy Carter McDonald

Published By
Bluewater Publications

Table of Contents

Paths in The Brier Patch
2nd Edition

By Dr. William Lindsey McDonald
Illustrated by Dorothy Carter McDonald

Hauling Logs

It takes a whole lot of cutting, hauling, and stacking to keep a wood fire burning. But it's worth all the hard work you put into it. As I look back across many years it seems a good portion of my labor has been with axe in hand. Mother's big woodbox at the back of the stove, it seemed, was surely without a bottom.

In those early years we had a homespun concept of economic evaluation. Nobody in our community owned stocks or bonds, or had anything in the bank. And you couldn't gauge a man's status by the car he drove, or the position he occupied, and much less by the clothes he wore. Yet, we were able to do a lot of guessing by looking at woodpiles. We admired industrious neighbors who had neat

cords of firewood cut and ready for winter by the first of fall. But he who put off this important chore until the last minute was immediately suspected of being lazy. I grew up convinced that unless I worked hard folks would joke about me as they did old man John. That poor fellow was never known to cut a stick of wood until the weather turned so cold that he looked miserable shivering over his chopping block.

I got my apprenticeship in felling trees and sawing logs at Daddy's farm in Tennessee. We learned there the mathematics of the cord and rick, and just where to lay the axe to make sure of a good split. But the most valuable lesson of all would be difficult to explain to those who have never worked except for salaries on a dollar scale. For one of life's most rewarding recompenses is an ache in your bones at the end of a day when you see gratifying results of a job well done that was worthy of all your exhaustion.

Now when I haul firewood and grow weary and declare I'm just not up to it, I stop and remember to give thanks and hope that I'll always be able to give a full day's work and to carry my share of the load. For, if someone's around to measure my worth...I'd be happy to know that he saw that I've been pretty busy splitting logs.

Our Farm

The home where we live was once a part of our farm. It provided food, clothes, and other necessities for several generations of my wife's family. I'm glad that I, too, planted its land and watched things grow. Our roots are deeply buried in this rich and fertile soil.

The city encircles what were once pastures and fields and wooded lots. Our dwindling acres are now a small island of tangled woods. Business houses moved from downtown environs to what was then rural countryside. Lanes of ever-circling traffic hem us in with mixed-up sounds of engines, transmissions and steel belted tires. Multiplying subdivisions have encroached upon sections where sorghum was planted, corn was harvested, and cattle once grazed.

Men are prone to label this expansion as progress and development. But we who were caught up in this change of lovely nature into asphalt and concrete know it as tragedy and desecration.

The transition came quietly and slowly. And this was merciful. Although man becomes accustomed to change, it somehow is easier when it does not all come at once.

A stable and tack room are fading reminders of animals that we once thought would belong always to the old place. How refreshing to remember their individual personalities and the quaint names we called them! Somehow, the joy of their birth and the sorrow of their death helped prepare us for the things that have since become ours to face.

Our barn gave way to a new road where strangers became our neighbors. I find it difficult adjusting to not having this big rambling old building. Nothing can replace its atmosphere of aging timbers...the fragrance of its hay bales...the sound of cows eating in the stalls...and the warmth of shiny leather hanging all around.

It is true that most of us fail to appreciate what we have and fully know its worth until we lose it. And then we never forget.

A Moment of Truth

I have a friend who practices law in upstate New York. Contrary to his profession he is a shy and unimposing fellow. A Major in the Army Reserves, he was my classmate at the Command and General Staff College in Kansas. The thing that made him really outstanding was the ribbon on his chest. He wore the Medal of Honor, our nation's highest award. The wearers of this decoration are not ordinary people. They are America's heroes who gave beyond the call of duty.

During a conversation at dinner one evening he revealed that he was that soldier who called for a direct air strike upon his own position in Vietnam. This almost certain death request made front pages around the country.

I asked how he felt when death seemed so imminent. "Reconciled," was his answer. And he added, "I was severely wounded already, and all the others with me were dead, and I thought I had no chance to live either way."

I shall not soon forget the other part of what he said: "Before then I did not believe in God. But that hour, as I faced the end, I met Him. I knew He cared, and I was not afraid. Miraculously I came away to live again. Now I believe God has a purpose for every life. And I'm trying the best I can to fill my role. "

And I thought how sometimes it takes a lifetime to learn what becomes a reality in a moment of truth.

Reflections Upon A Life That Lives

When I met him I knew he was a Champ. His six-foot or more frame and reddish sun-bleached hair and trim, yet muscular, appearance was that of an athlete. I could tell, too, by the way he carried himself. Every movement, every step had the mark of a winner.

That he was. Dedicated to a dream of perfection, he drove himself in practice and drill and work and toil to fulfill that goal, and won.

I've been thinking about this boy and the things he stood for and the goals he fought for, and that which he left with us.

I ride by and look at his creek-his by right of conquest. His ancestors tilled their crops on the banks of these waters. But he saw the same creek with a new perspective and dared to challenge its waves and wind and depths. With boat and ski and determination he launched out and won.

I knew him only briefly. Yet, I was amazed at the fullness of his knowledge. I talked with him and came away impressed with what he knew about any subject ranging from sports to world events, from the ancient arts to modern science, and just about anything else you cared to mention. It was obvious that he had made other goals and in his masterful way won them as well.

But that which he worked hardest to attain became his highest achievement. In retrospect one wonders if maybe unconsciously he knew his allotted years would be few. For indeed he gave every day the very best of himself in a special sort of way that mingled a wealth of happiness with a whole lot of wholesomeness to leave forever a light that cannot be dimmed and a joy that cannot be fathomed.

How glad we are that Reggie Fullerton lived. For his life, though brief in quantity, was full in quality and was not in vain. He dared to be great and was and is and will be forever. He played to win and won.

That's really what life is all about. "They that go down to the sea in ships that do business in great waters: These see the works of the Lord, and his wonders in the deep."

Fireflies And A Summer's Night

The firefly is one of nature's multi-wonders. This prehistoric insect flits about in ways it did during the age of dinosaurs. It is a masterful combination of art and science- landscape architect, electrical engineer, environmentalist and chemist. It probably holds a secret formula for man's modern quest for energy conservation as well as a solution for an environmental problem. This harmless little creature furnishes practically heatless light by oxidation of a pigment in luminescent organisms that perpetuates itself through cycles of death and birth.

It is impossible to count their lights in the grass and boxwood and reach the grand canopy of tall trees. I'm delighted they are here to add charm and grace and enchantment to a summer's night.

I'm glad, too, they never change and are always the same. Once I chased them to put into a jar. Now I watch and wish that life somehow could be as simple and carefree again.

But the nocturnal fly flickers this night and the soft darkness is turned into a carnival of fun and mystery. Looking across the lawn filled with thousands of ageless lights I know, too, that there are some things that will never change. And He who created man and fly is the same yesterday, today, and forever.

Subdivisions And Landmarks

Grandpa's been gone a long time. But the house he built still lingers at the crest of his hill. Houses are not built his way anymore. We now develop subdivisions that articulate an atmosphere of luxury, comfort, and conformity. Grandpa was not one to consider ordering a blueprint, or copying a design from a book or magazine. His rooms were not arranged according to familiar patterns, and he was not one to place a hall where it was not needed. He knew what he wanted, and built it.

And it became a conspicuous site used by neighbors to mark directions to locate other places. It doesn't take a mansion, or the birth of a famous person, or the signing of an important treaty, to make a house into a landmark.

There is something about the unusual style of this old structure that silently speaks of the one who built it. Grandpa was his own man. It would have been foreign to his nature to think as others thought, or dress as neighbors dressed, or to be overly concerned about what they said. He spoke when he figured he should take a stand, and never hesitated to be himself.

Man, like fashionable houses, now orients himself to the subdivision. Generally, we take our cues from others to strive to be like them. Society punctuates our speeches, and determines what we wear, and the notion of the masses sets our feet in the same direction.

But a man, like a landmark, is best remembered when he dares to be different.

Moving Bicycles

I've been thinking about all the trimming and mowing around the yard that needs to be done now that Spring is here. But there is one function I already miss...moving bicycles. Let me tell you, there was a time, and only a few years back, when this was my pet peeve. Our girls always would leave those mechanical whizzes right in my way, on the patio, walkway and drive. How irritating it was to go about the place moving those bicycles.

But now there are no bicycles. How tidy the yard is and how strangely silent, too. I have a belated confession. Moving bicycles was fun. But I didn't know about the fun part back when it was a pet peeve.

I'd dearly love to move a bicycle today. I long for just one to be in my way. And before moving it, I would sit down and enjoy again the laughter of happy children at play. I'd see the beauty and not the clutter. I'd drink up those golden moments of yesterday that I was too busy to enjoy.

I'd gladly trade my tidy yard and the silence of the trees for swings that hang from limbs, and laughter that livens up the place, and for bicycles that are in my way.

Summer's Ending

Summer came only a short while ago. And ushered in what seemed to be a time to slacken our pace and to take some time away from work and all the other things that keep us running day and night. Man needs moments to be alone...for rest...with no thought of urgent and pressing matters.

Summer's beginnings in June were closely mixed with a freshness of flowers and ripening of vegetables. It did seem then that August would be a long time coming.

Those sun-filled, hot, dry days came and went. Now another season has about run its quick and allotted course. We can see and feel the beginnings of the end; the night air changes, and the sky begins to take on the deeper blue of another season.

Outdoor grills for hamburgers and such soon will be folded and stored, vacation lands will become pretty pictures posted in scrapbooks, and the school bus will bring sudden silence to playgrounds, baseball fields, picnic parks, and swimming pools.

I had many plans for this vacation season...but in the busy circle of things, I didn't find the time. And now it's too late. I forgot the axiom, "the time to relax is when you don't have time for it."

I did not remember that summers don't last as long as they used to...not nearly as long as they did when I wore knee breeches and swam in worn pants that mother made into swimming trunks.

Times have changed. Things have changed. We have changed. But those of us who are too busy to capture a small and beautiful part of summer are just too busy.

Unselfish Gifts Of Love

We called him Pop, because he was older than the rest of us who had been drafted out of high school. He had done a little more living; we were new in the business.

Moving through cold darkness before dawn we collected our three-day rations at Le Harve, France, and boarded an old antique train to cut our way through heavy snow into Belgium.

Our meager rations were stored at one end of the car. There would be no more until we got to where we were going.

We warned Pop. But he couldn't resist giving his food away at every crossing along the way. Little hungry faces reminded him of his own back home, and their outstretched hands were rewarded that day.

We felt sorry for Pop that night when eagerly we reached for our supply. But we found nothing at all in our boxes. Pop had given away all of his rations and ours as well.

Gnawing hunger pains the next couple of days did not help our sympathy for this lover of children. It has been a long time since he gave away our food, and I guess the rest of us have thought about it a lot; at least I have. You see, I have children of my own now, and I understand and am ashamed of my own selfishness.

It's not too hard to give when you expect something in return. And it's easy to love when you are loved. Pop gave with love to those he would never see again.

I have been thinking of the kinds of love I have seen. And I've yet to see love more genuine and more beautiful than this father who saw in every child his very own. Better I understand the love of God and His gift of His Son.

The Old House

I knew I should not go. But last week I went to the scene of yesterday and stood once more looking at the big house that Papa Johnson built. This was my last look. You see, next week, and forever after, it will be only a memory of what once was and will never be again.

I tried to remember happy times in that old house. I looked hard but could not tell where Mama's roses had been when I was a boy. Pleasant memories dance in my head when I see a rose; Mama's would bloom in the spring all the way across the two-storied front porch. I searched for Aunt Maggie's sweet shrub that filled the air with mystic perfume on those comforting nights when our old folks sat out front in the rows of swings and gliders and rocking chairs.

I tried to remember, but all I could see was nothingness. All I could hear was the breaking of boards and the crashing of timbers thrown aimlessly to the forsaken ground. These wreckers were ruthless in their onslaught. But they could not know the gentle people who once lived among those walls.

A numb pain ached in my body and gripped my soul. I turned and walked away and knew I could never come this way again.

The World is Shrinking

Pretty dolls of every color and style and from every continent on the globe were singing a lively and catchy song, "It's a Small, Small, World." Of all the attractions in California's Disneyland, I remember the sound of this music best of all. In fact, the more I travel, and see and hear, the more I find myself unconsciously thinking about their theme, and sometimes even humming their tune.

Science, technology, satellite communications, and space explorations have expanded horizons and reduced distances. During the Second World War we crossed the Atlantic on the USS *Zassar Victory* in eleven long and drawn-out days. Now, I can eat supper in New York and breakfast the next morning in London, or Paris, or Rome.

Yesterday I left Alabama following a hearty breakfast...had supper and slept comfortably last night in a motel that overlooked Stage Junction, Virginia. In 1824, my ancestors left this place in March and arrived at Elk River in Alabama around the middle of June. They came by covered wagons and stopped along the way to bury a child, and to give birth to another.

Just a little while ago I met Frank Luttrell of Louisville, Kentucky. Now, this stranger didn't mean anything to me-not until he introduced himself and said that we knew each other many years ago at old Camp Pendleton.

It is a small, small world. We follow yesterday's trails-but with almost unbelievable speed and in comfort that many times is more luxurious than home. We sometimes meet forgotten friends from the past. And frequently run into neighbors many miles from home. And we are always happy when we encounter strangers who know or claim kin to folks we know.

This morning I passed by the home of Mrs. Olivia Waltonin Charlottesville, Virginia. She is the real-life mother of the popular television family series, "The Waltons."

Neighbors told me of her frustrations. People visit her from all over the world. Tourists crowd her street day and night. They even tore down her picket fence and carried it away piece by piece. Telephone operators have to screen her phone calls for protection. And Mrs. Walton longs for solitude and privacy and a normal life.

Life in a shrinking world can become complicated and complex and can present many problems. Man can no longer live even close to old patterns of the past. We soon learn that there are now no islands where man can escape, and life will never be a vacuum.

Ours is a small world. And it's a beautiful place to be. And today is the most exciting time to live. I think I would not have wanted to miss it-not for anything, ever!

Reunion

The few old, faded photographs were almost deceptive. The young faces with boyish grins could have fit into any highschool yearbook. Yet the olive-drab clothing and the stark background told a different story. These pictures were not from an ordinary era. Those in the photographs were caught up by a destiny that brought them together in a place far removed from the comfort and security of campus and home.

We were those boys. And, now, after more than three decades, we were together again, this time on the serene shores of Smith's Mountain Lake, not far from television's celebrated Walton's Mountain in Virginia.

I guess we were all aware that there had been a lot of changes. Ed resembled his early image more than the rest. He is still tall, slim, and quiet. But the salt-and-pepper gray in his unmilitary sideburns revealed the passing of years. I would not have known Earle, except for his distinguished voice. And I do believe this will be his recognizable feature a hundred years from today. Some things never change. But when I glanced at a mirror on the wall, I knew that "Ole Alabama" had not only changed-those years had been more severe with him than the others.

Ed Fitzgerald and his lovely family opened up their vacation cottage, fed us T-bone steaks, rode us about on the lake, and gave us a tour of the mountain heights. As Brooks so well said, everything was fantastic.

And I don't like to say goodbye. That's why I tiptoed out of the cottage and drove away from the mountain and lake before the moon went down and the sun came up.

I met a deer on the winding road and saw a jet-black squirrel drinking at a small fountain that nature carved with a spring that dripped from a rocky ridge into a pool beside the highway.

I bathed my soul in a beautiful world that is always at the breaking of every dawn. And I thought of other days, and my old friends, and I wondered if we would ever meet again.

Enough For Us And The Crows

Often I reminisce about events and people and times not to be again. And I remember lessons learned in simple and meaningful ways. Back in other years my neighbor joined me in planting a crop of corn. After the work of plowing and sowing I began my usual worries about the crows. Each morning the endless chatter of these scavengers increased my fears. Surely, they were taking away all we had put into the ground!

Early one morning with loaded shotgun I made my way through damp weeds to scatter the birds and save what little might have been left. Nearing the field I was startled to see my farmer friend standing in his characteristically placid way obviously enjoying what to me was a calamity. Lee grinned at my rude approach and asked what I was doing with that gun. I told him I was sure we had already lost our crop.

I'll never forget his reasonable advice: "No need to worry! When I set that planter, I made sure there would be enough for both us and the crows." And when harvest time came, sure enough, we had plenty-in spite of those thieving birds.

Our lives sometimes become cumbered with cares and concern over little things that never happen at all. Our faith can provide for good times and hard times when we trust in a Provider who cares for sparrows as well as man.

Baseball Comes With Spring

As Californians count Spring by the sparrows at Capistrano, baseball is my private comfort for the arrival of this wonderful season. The slow pace of this warm weather game is in contrast to the fast action of football and basketball and the energy-burning demands for cold and clammy nights. Football speaks of frost, and basketball of snow. But baseball brings a peaceful flavor of Spring breezes, and lazy hot summer evenings.

I do believe that one of life's better moments is the radio broadcasting of the first exhibition game before the season gets underway. They call it the grapefruit league, but to me it is a remembering time for games played long ago. The deliberate pace of the announcer gives time to reminisce the ruddy faces with hearty laughter of boyhood friends-and wonder where they went.

Charlie Brown is my favorite funny-page character. I guess it's because he never wins a game. It's easy to identify past failures with him. Charles Schulz, cartoonist, must have known a lot about how it is to grow up as an average kind of boy.

Someone observed that Babe Ruth hit 714 home runs-and struck out 1,440 times. People forgot his failures, but never forgot his victories.

I don't think we won many times in our hollow. The other side seemed always to have the better team. But that doesn't matter now. Who would remember the score? The thing that counts is that we loved the game, and there were some mighty fine fellows that made up our team.

It's easy to become bogged down in the technicalities of scores and wins and losses. But I believe there's a lot of truth in the adage, "It's how well you play the game."

A sportsman, confident he had played the game well, wrote a long time ago:

I have fought a good fight

I have finished my course....

And as I look back at games past, and ahead to games yet to be played, I know in my heart that giving all you have is really what matters.

Old Dogged Daddy Pat

We would have gladly followed him through the paths of Dante's *Inferno*. He was that kind of man-a man's man, a soldier among soldiers, a born leader, and one in whose hands we never feared to place our lives. He was our commander in the Korean War, a Lieutenant Colonel. We called him "Daddy Pat." But never to his face. This title was that of respect and genuine affection.

Daddy Pat was always aloof, staying mostly to himself, and no one dared invade his private world. He was Irish, a devoted Catholic, small in stature, very thin, but had eyes of steel that pierced man and machine. He possessed a bear-trap memory, never forgot a name. One day he startled a newcomer by calling him Jim. When asked how he knew, the old man replied, "Why, don't you remember? We met at a road block in Belgium during the Battle of the Bulge."

The thing we most admired about old Pat was his persistent determination. Nothing was impossible. He said it just took a little longer to do the impossible. And woe to that officer who said it can't be done. Fact is, I never knew anyone in the old man's command who dared think such a thought.

Another characteristic that won our respect was the fierce way he backed us. He would fight a lion for his men. And he did. Old Pat would stand behind us in any decision; but as sure as shooting we had better be right. He never tolerated anything short of the very best.

I knelt with old Pat one day beside a man who had been shot. He had a hole in his chest big enough for my hand to go through. I didn't know until then that strong men cried. They do. I saw tears in the old man's eyes.

I've been thinking a lot lately about a lot of things going on about us. Most of the trouble and problems are brought about by those weak and without principles, who are wishy-washy in character, and never take a stand for the right.

Sometimes I turn off my television set and ponder how different the world would be if we had a few old dogged Daddy Pats around. One thing for certain, I surely would sleep a lot easier tonight.

All The Christmases Yet To Be

Highly pleasing, pretty, and clever little stories are part of our children's television heritage during holiday seasons. My grandchildren count hours and eagerly anticipate these Santaland tales. It's also a lot of fun for an old man like me to get caught up in the delightful enchantment of the youngest generation.

The biggest part of my entertainment, though, is watching expressions of little ones as they catch the sensation of the miracle that has captured the imagination of children for almost two thousand years.

I wondered tonight if the keeping of this wonderful ceremony will change as much for this little four-year-old girl, and that tall six-year-old boy, as it has during my lifetime. Christmas remains the same, but the ways I knew it would be unfamiliar to excited eyes in a land of sophisticated space toys and almost human dolls.

We little boys hoped for one real toy, and couldn't wait to show it to all our kin who were coming and going...for it was always a family day at my Daddy's place. And think of the difference in the Florida orange in these last fifty years. It's a common thing now, but it surely was a fantastic find in my stocking hung by the chimney...along with red apples, English walnuts, raisins, and the colorful array of peppermint and hard rock candies. I'm overwhelmed with the abundance of modern decorations...ours were so simple...and yet I remember them the most.

Now is the day of the splendid spruce and pine that can be bought at the shopping center. We went to the woods for ours. And my preference for decorated trees will always be that stately and magnificent cedar...for long ago the fragrance of its branches became forever a part of all the festivities of the holidays.

Seems there is a mountain of yuletide goodies now; always dishes, cakes, and cookies that need our tasting. But back then, for me, will always be the best...delicate ambrosia, honest-to-goodness cornbread dressing with no more than a pinch of sage, coconut cake served with 'po man's sauce.' Those were the days. But I have to admit that Christmas at any age is hard to beat.

I dare not guess what the future will be. It is not within my powers to predict or even speculate on the changing styles these grandchildren will know in their tomorrow. But I do believe that it will be well in a world that takes time to find the magic of this season...and to know the meaning and the true Spirit of all the Christmases yet to be.

Two Men, Spoken Words, & A Song

Two men died recently. Both moved in circles I've never known. They were associated with the Metropolitan Opera I've never seen. I had never met them. Yet, both gave me something of inestimable worth.

Milton Cross was the radio commentator for the Opera as long as I can remember. I was intrigued by his sonorous voice and his perfection with words. His careful and deliberate pronunciation reflected a personality that seemed to reach out to touch and give pleasure.

I learned from this man that a well-spoken word is the essential ingredient of conversation. And without it, speech is garbled into many confusing symbols. Through his use of the English language he showed that dignity is an indefinable quality which is a part of character and that one of its distinguishing features is simplicity.

The voice of Milton Cross gave me an inspiration. I know I shall never attain any measure of his ability with the simple spoken word. But I must try!

Richard Tucker was the leading singer for thirty years with the Metropolitan Opera. He was considered the best American tenor of his time, if not the best in the world. Through the influence of a friend, I had the opportunity not long ago of attending a concert of Richard Tucker at the Kennedy Center of Fine Arts in Washington. I was enchanted at the uncanny consistency and durability of the voice of this short, stocky, barrel-chested singer who looked more like an aged football player.

At the close of his high-caliber performance, in response to the standing demand of the audience, he came back to give an encore. It was a song of simple words written for a Broadway performance. He forged these words into a dynamo of challenge and strength. His voice gave life to a song. This song spoke of the impossible dream, the righting of wrongs, the unreachable star. These words to an unforgettable song have inspired me in my business of striving; these two men personify the glorious quest.

February; The Hard Month

One hardly knows whether to expect wind or balm, rain or snow, or a biting cold, or a warm and welcomed sun. The ancients called it Mud Month. But they couldn't have experienced a December and January with the mud we had this winter.

February stands out in many ways. One is because it has less days than any other month. In fact, it was robbed. Originally, the Roman calendar allotted it twenty-nine days. But after Augustus Caesar named August for himself, he became upset because his month had only thirty days; whereas July, named for his uncle Julius Caesar, had thirty-one. So, he ordered another day removed from already short February, and added it to August so he would be equal to Uncle Julius.

A strange phenomenon occurred in February, 1866. There was no full moon. Astronomers said it had never happened before and would not occur again for two and a half million years. If there is a best month to be born in, then history can give a lot of weight to February.

The Cherokees called this month Hunger Moon, and said that if they could get through this lean and hard phase of their moon-oriented calendar year they had it made for the other seasons.

Maybe being the last full month of winter is responsible for this feeling for February. Its weather is often deceitful. One day can bring a lull of false Spring; whereas, the next can be so brutal that the early crocus and daffodils are bitten by frost or ice. But, granting that this month surely seems hard and requires extra effort to get through, we would be at a disadvantage without our Februaries.

John Ruskin, the English art critic of the last century, once wrote that one of the big calamities of his life was that he had it too easy. He was born into wealth and never knew danger and pain and the struggles of going without...or fighting for the necessities of survival.

To my way of thinking, it takes hard licks, disappointments, failures, and sorrows to strengthen our moral fiber and to give us the zest for life.

We need our Februaries. Oft-times it is necessary to grit our teeth and drive straight down the middle. But Spring waits on the other side.

A Happy Man

It has another name. But I call the place "apple valley." There is no better description for this lovely dale tucked snugly among the misty heights of the Blue Ridge Mountains. Orchards dominate as living architecture. They cleave tenaciously to steep slopes and bid a hearty welcome to tired and lonely wanderers passing along the way.

Autumn brings out baskets of their many-colored fruits stacked in rows from one end of the valley to the other. Nowhere has the handiwork of the Master Painter been more artistically exhibited than among these hills and hollows and trees and crates of red and golden apples.

A hand-lettered, roadside advertisement proved more than I could resist..."Eat 'em, Bake 'em, Fry 'em, Apple Pie 'em.', And Charlie Goolrich, who printed this sign and planted thirty-six acres of seeds twenty-seven years ago, proudly presented me with samples of every kind from his family grove. He claimed they represent all the varieties grown in the State of the Old Dominion...the Red Delicious, Golden Delicious, Stayman, Winesap, Rome and the York.

Now Charlie surely knows all there is to know about apples. It's an education to hear this twiny little fellow, who resembles the trunk of his pruned trees, exclaim with excitement their fancies and advantages. One cannot but go away to become a great enthusiast of these fruits, and touched by the enthusiasm of the one who grows and sells them.

How refreshing in these times to meet a man who believes in what he is doing, loves his work, and is convinced that his apples are special and the best that money can buy! How sad our plight when chained to what we have made unpleasant and unbearable by the attitude we labor under.

To my way of thinking, a lot of folks merely work to exist, rather than put their life into the joy of the work. There aren't many Charlie Goolrichs left. But when you find his kind you have found a truly happy man.

The Girl On A Horse

She rode into my life as a fresh breeze on a hot summer's day. Bubbling with personality and winsome in manners, she introduced herself and asked permission to ride through our woods and around our pasture. She quickly became a part of our place, gracing the trees and bridle paths.

Often I found myself glancing about, hoping to catch a glimpse of the splash of sunshine that brought back youth and merriment to long silenced fences and gates and barns. How glad we were that she chose our place to ride her horse.

Yesterday she rode away from our woods and our pasture and our lives. Our small patch of land must seem insignificant to her now, as she rides in search of the wind and the stars, among bridle paths that are unending, and on grass that is eternally green. But our trees and paths and lives have been enriched because the girl on a horse rode our way for a brief season. I'm thinking how this stark tragedy we face is yet so much a part of life as we know it.

Briefly we meet to love and laugh and weep, and all too quickly we ride away. Give or take an eon or two, it matters not how few or how many our years may be; but what does matter is what we do with the time we have, and what we leave behind when we ride away.
I wonder.

The girl on a horse left us with renewed visions of a better day, and with a memory of a youth with wholesome values in a troubled and complex age. You see, we have hopes for our tomorrow when we know wholesomeness and purity and beauty as we saw in the girl on a horse who rode through our woods and about our pasture.

She rode away and left a whole lot of sunshine behind. [A memorial to our neighbor, Miss Connie Carol James. Who died in 1972.]

Poke Sallet

I've looked around old fence rows today, gathering fresh green shoots of the delight of the South. Poke sallet is as much a part of Spring as the robin and lilac. It's a good spring tonic, rich in iron, vitamin C, phosphorus and other minerals. And according to an authority in Old English at the University, it has to be spelled "sallet," and not "salad."

Cooked just right, in eggs, onions, and with salt pork or bacon drippings, it is an epicurean's dish of homespun delight. Have yet to discover a more gourmet food, when eaten with cornbread, green onions, and a glass of buttermilk. This is a feast that annually celebrates a pleasing end to the monotony of winter's meals.

I suppose if one lives in the city he will need to come to the rural areas to find them. Yet, it's hard for the man of the country to think there could be a place on earth where this plant dares not grow.

I've never laid claims to any laurels in cooking. But the art of eating is yet another story. However, for kicks, in more carefree college days I took an elective course in home economics. Things didn't go as expected, and it was a more difficult task than led to believe, but I completed the class with a prize-winning recipe called "poke sallet in a skillet." But this was not original; it was a hand-me-down from Mother and Grandma and, no doubt, from generations before them.

It's always worth the trip and time to pick these plants of the wild and prepare them for the table. The roots of the poke weed are poisonous, and should be trimmed away, along with the thick stems and poor leaves. The remaining should be washed and rinsed in cool clear water, boiled twice, and then combined with onions in bacon drippings; eggs are stirred in immediately before taken off the heat.

The story of this ordinary weed is a saga of frontier times. It would have remained an unsightly growth and a nuisance to cultivation had the Scotch-Irish of the Southern Appalachians not known hardship and bare survival.

It reminds us that in the hidden mysteries of nature there is good and beauty in all things, no matter how common.

The Wedding

We walked down the aisle tonight, my youngest daughter and I. Her long and flowing white gown accentuated a dark complexion and radiant beauty. The veil she wore covered, but could not conceal, the happiness I saw in wide and exciting blue eyes. This was my little princess turned now into a pretty bride...the one everyone had come to see...and the center of the total concentration and attention of the young man waiting at the altar. My one and only solemn and considerable duty at this time was to give her away and sit down.

The distance seemed longer and more exhausting than it had first appeared. The correct and proper military bearing... learned during days in ceremonies of pomp and parade years before my child was born...had deserted me at a time I needed it most. All the training exercised in the old Corps," to be prepared to assume command of any situation," was now hopelessly beyond my ability to try to carry out. For I found myself bowed under a weight of long-gone events while remembering things that will be no more.

I saw days and months and years that had passed so fast and wondered where they had gone. I heard once more an exciting mixture of childhood and teenage voices and desperately tried, but failed, to place them in their proper sequence. I wondered why we sometimes neglect the appreciation of all the inestimable moments in life until we see finally they are ours no more.

A new home was established under soft and sacred lights this night. This magnificent old sanctuary, built in another era with an ageless dignity, and adorned with the art of a prayerful people, is symbolic of the blessings I ask for my daughter and my new son.

May their marriage be a haven of peace, founded and sustained upon that faith and communion of their fathers in ages past, and undergirded with constant trust and hope in the Father of all mankind. For our Creator is not confined to a short and limited distance as has been my lot to go, but He shall walk with them all the way...in sickness and in health...in sorrow and in joy...in life and in death.

Autumn In The Country

Summer leaves reluctantly, as a guest who had rather not go. But what remains of summer mingles with autumn into an atmosphere of beauty and tranquility found at no other season. Noah, they say, began loading his ark on the 30th of October in some not-specified year, and that's something to think about. This was to give the world a new beginning. And that's a beautiful thought as our days grow shorter and our evenings longer. Winter is ahead, but so, too, is spring, with its flowers and leaves and life.

Fall is extremely different from spring. After all, what could contrast more with violent March than the gentle morning mist of October, shot through with shafts of sun among the cedars? And winter is a contrast too; now the trees are not just skeletal designs, waving in cold wind, but drip with soft shades of yellow, rust and brown...the raked leaves are pungent with damp earth...the scarlet sumac is suddenly there around the bend...the hunter's moon hangs over mown fields and sunshine constantly mingles with gently falling leaves.

Autumn is no ending of the year and should bring no feeling of finality. There is so much glory in this short season that we should do as the busy animals of the woods and fields, and store up what we manage to capture of its atmosphere. We can then recall at will all the fragrant nostalgia, the rare glimpse of wild geese, the southwest slant of evening sun, the drone of mowing in the fields, the last warm tomato from the vine, the depth of blue sky over sparkling frost, the rhythmic drip of rain, the log fire and popcorn and quilts at night.

Other seasons have their unique traits, but most of all we feel the need of Autumn's peace. And so we can bring it out of our storehouse at any time...to bask in the glow that only it can give.

The Porch

I have lived a lot on porches. And grew up where one was in front and another at the back. In designing our present house, we finally compromised on a leisure-type side veranda. A house seemed to be incomplete without this that had always been a part of me.

Porches went out of style about the time carports became the vogue. But I guess the real causes for the demise of this architectural appendage were its high costs and our modern-day air conditioners.

The porch at our old homeplace was our sanctuary for shade that seemed always to guarantee a breeze even in the hottest of weather. But it was more than a cooling-off room. Half of the year it served as Mother's parlor.

All our kin and neighbors were entertained and served a glass of iced tea in this pleasant place. In the evenings when supper was over we would all retire to the swing and rockers waiting out front.

My earliest recollections of Grandmother are associated with this swing. Here she spun exciting stories of olden times that whetted my appetite for history, and my earliest attempts at writing. My boyhood ambition was to record all she said so that someday I could share her wonderland of stories with my own grandchildren.

I think I must have planned my life on the front porch. As I look back now I realize that most of the big milestones, like college and things, were laid out first in daydreams that grew into goals. And surely one could not find a place more conducive to planning than the peace afforded a growing boy in the open air of the family porch.

I'm not qualified to pass out too much advice. I leave that to others with their specialized professions. But I think a lot of living was sacrificed when they did away with the old front porch.

Gardens And Light Thought

Tomatoes have been good this summer, our corn fair, and practically no bean harvest at all. Most folk lay it to the weather. Rain has been inconsistent, and during the heart of the growing season the earth was dry. Yet, to be philosophical about it, our gardens, like most everything else in life, depend largely upon the amount of work we put into them. A poor singer doesn't prove the song is bad. But the same can't be said for a lazy gardener.

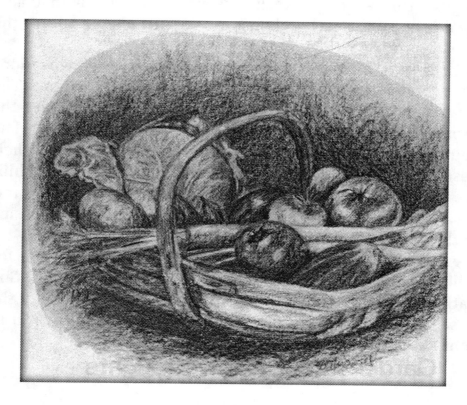

We miss our neighbor's garden and his smiling approval of growing things. I never knew him to fail. Good seasons and bad seasons alike produced the best for him. Lee Springer had a green thumb, or so they said. But I knew differently. It was plenty of good, honest hard work. And he enjoyed every day of it. Lee could make a rosebush bloom after everybody else quit trying. He was a man of such enduring character that his death was like losing a great tree or a river.

We had a bumper crop of black-eyed peas. Preacher Tom Kitchens used to say that I ate peas like a whippoorwill. And of all vegetables they are the best when cooked with a little pork. These small peas revolutionized our table fork. The English three-pronged fork was not workable with black-eyed peas, so the early colonist Americanized it by adding the fourth prong.

History has been changed by crop failures. Civilizations have prospered and vanished around staple plants. The Scotch and Irish potato blights from 1782 to 1846 sent the proud Highlanders from Europe to the Carolinas. The Southern Appalachian is made up mostly of their descendants. I often think about how much richer these hills are because of those disastrous crop failures of another time. A catastrophe for one generation can prove to be a blessing to the next.

August is a fine month, fine for eating vegetables, for lolling in the shade, and for thinking light thoughts. But God hath chosen the foolish things of the world to confound the wise; and God hath chosen the weak things of the world to confound the things which are mighty...

A Delightful Surprise

I've been thinking of the multi-ways we depend upon energy and how fantastic its acceleration during my lifetime. Grandpa owned the only car in our family. It was a special occasion to visit in the evening where there was a radio. The momentous event we never forgot was the day TVA connected the power that brought abundant light into the old homeplace.

Mother had the first refrigerator on our hill, and the nearest telephone was at Aunt Maggie's in the valley below. Now, all of these and a hundred other gadgets are considered not luxuries...but the basic essentials of twentieth-century living.

In looking for ways to save our rapidly depleting vital resources, my family recently retreated several decades to the outmoded clothesline in the back yard. But we call it by the new and apt name...solar drying.

It saves use of electricity that is generated mostly from coal...and utilizes rays from the sun that otherwise would not be captured if clothes were not hanging out to dry. But our delightful surprise was the overwhelming freshness of things when dried by a scorching sun. We had forgotten during more convenient years all of the good things that can come from more simple ways.

There are some labor-savers I would not wish to give up. I remember too well the hard chores of washing the big iron pot, and hauling water in a bucket, and splitting wood for the kitchen stove. But, I think, to sacrifice a few of our modern appliances may well give back pleasant experiences once known and lost.

Most everyone agrees that we ride too much and walk too little. Long before the energy crisis I found a few dividends by leaving the car in the garage whenever possible. Walking helps the circulation, keeps a better trim on the waistline, and makes for more restful sleep at night.

We Americans are a funny lot. We work hard for our right to be free and yet become enslaved to gadgets and things. It takes a major crisis or even a disaster sometimes to bring us to our proper perspective. But once faced with what has to be done, these unique people called Americans...anointed seems with a special power called "Yankee ingenuity"...have always found a way to do it.

Pumpkins And Things

This is the time of year some people can enjoy the satisfying feeling that comes from looking at their own pumpkin patch. If you've never raised pumpkins and things that grow there is no way to describe what it's like when the labor is over and the harvest is ready.

There are a whole lot of lessons to be learned from the ordinary pumpkin. Its ungainly appearance is a stark contrast to the tender and delicate rose. This loveliest of all nature's flowers has been cross-bred and perfected into many enchanting varieties. Yet, the pumpkin, kin to the squash and gourd, is not so cooperative with the science of horticulture. Even if cross-pollination is successful, its fruit doesn't easily revert to ordinary reproduction.

So, it seems, the pumpkin is one thing that's hard to change from what it has always been. They are larger than their ancestors. And some think this may be the only significant improvement since they were first cultivated by the ancient Indians in Central America. Although they make good fodder, they are best known for jack-o'lanterns at Halloween. But their best use, as far as I'm concerned, is making them into hot, spicy pies by someone who knows exactly how.

A field of yellow pumpkins can do a lot for a man's thinking and his sense of values. By some means it seems to change an exhausting day into one that reveals how much a day is really worth.

Looking at a common pumpkin patch can even momentarily change a man into a boy again and cause him to wonder if things would be different if he had a chance to begin anew. Some folks spend a lot of time thinking and writing about theology. I'd rather plant, and see things grow, and reflect now and then about these simple ways. Then I can better understand what little I'm given to know about the One who took the time and effort to create inelegant and yet satisfying things as squashes, gourds and pumpkins.

Ringing The Bell

Many wonderful memories of my childhood are centered in the old church that stood as a landmark in the hollow below our house. Long ago it burned to ashes on a cold winter night. A beautiful edifice was soon erected among the ruins. But it could never replace the building where I had gathered so much of life in those growing boyhood days.

My grandfather would take me there. We would arrive so early that it seems we watched forever for each service to begin. But during these waits, and before all others arrived, Uncle Henry would faithfully come and ring the bell. This kind and quiet and ancient little man had been the bell ringer for as long as anybody could remember. I grew up thinking that he held the most important position in the congregation; not even the preacher with his eloquent sermon could surpass that paramount task of ringing the church bell.

Uncle Henry was slow and deliberate. He went about his job in such a way that created within me a fervent wish. For I wanted, more than anything in all the world, to pull that rope and sound that clarion call up the hollow and across the hills. One day my dream became a reality. The dedicated keeper of the bell sent word that the only way he would consent to be away on that Sunday was conditioned upon my accepting the awesome responsibility. I have never been entrusted with a more exciting and honored task. And I'm sure, in thinking back, that the old man must have read what was in a young boy's eyes.

There was no sleep the night before; and I was at Grandpa's house the next morning even before he was ready. At church we pulled up chairs to wait. Granddaddy held his gold watch so we could count the hour, the minutes, and seconds. It seemed the moment would never arrive! But, at last, I heard my grandpa say, "Son, it's time to ring the bell."

It's difficult to describe the rapture of that instant when with eager hands I pulled the rope. A hundred bands and a thousand voices could not equal the music I heard that morning as I yanked and strained and the bell clanged its call to worship.

Across these many years I still get excited when thinking about that bell. Sometimes when I stand alone and am discouraged and wo-nder how I can find strength to carry on, I close my eyes and wander back through time to the little church un-der the hill. This memory has a way of righting my wrongs and renewing my strength. For it almost seems I hear Grandpa say, "Son, it's time to ring the bell."

A Message From Ashes

Have you wondered as I have about old houses? Even one abandoned that was once a home acquires an augury about it that permeates walls and floors and shingles. Seasons of sun and rain with neglect took its toll on our old house that long ago had been a home. Deterioration crept slowly but surely among rotting timbers, leaking roofs and unpainted finishings and left it a hull and no longer a house. We tried to hide its naked shame behind rows of bushes and hedges, but our guilt remained with its lifeless frame.

Our memories too long had lingered. We tried to keep it as it once had been. But our eyes were blinded to what was really taking place. Once this cottage, surrounded by lilac and larkspur, it was the pride of its builder. He planned, designed, and had it ready for his new bride on the day of their wedding.

It became a place where children grew, and life's earliest lessons were learned. It was a home for the best of love, a comfort in the worst of storms, and a wellspring of abundant blessings for all who entered its lighted doors. While the builder lived this house it lacked neither sacrifice of his valued time nor the exactness of his tender care. He kept it always in splendid repair. It was a humble dwelling endowed with an air of elegance. Everyone equally found comforting security blended with a warm welcome at its hearth and table.

Yet, the day the builder died signaled the beginning of the end for this that had been his life's dream. Aged houses do not fare well without a special measure of love and dedication. So, helpless and shorn of all its long-gone glory, our home of yesterday stood in silent suffering with an atmosphere of agony that seemed to plead for a time of relief and an hour of deliverance.

And as sometimes happens in the wonder of things we neither see nor understand, the hand of fate heard the pathetic cry. Lightning flashed, thunder rolled, and one tremendous bolt gave the death it so rightly deserved. And the frame hull that contained a half-century of memories went away in a final flame of glory.

Silently, we stood looking at the smoldering ashes. And I thought about how many things are worse than death and how much better for homes and men to die gracefully than to live in dishonor.

A Snow In The Shenandoah

The ground changed from umber to white as my car climbed the Blue Ridge. And going down into the Shenandoah, the weather unleashed sheets of blowing and whirling snow. Mike Houston loved to write about his valley- the great Shenandoah. Born and reared in Barboursville, he had a special brand of understanding. His writings in a rural journal were humanistic to the point that one could see, feel, and know as he did.

To read his descriptions of snow in his valley was to wish to be a part of that, too. This was my opportunity. I remembered his special nook at a small wayside cafe. They serve simple food in an atmosphere rarely found in these days of commercialization. I had to turn off the Interstate and drive about ten miles to find the place. And I don't believe I've enjoyed a more delightful supper. The ham was cured as only Virginians can do.

And snappy, hot biscuits were almost as good as those Mother used to bake. I sat facing a window glazed over with ice from the raging storm on the outside...the much more to make it comfortable and warm and friendly in the inn.

A thousand memories came my way in the priceless setting of tranquility. I reached for and held on to a few. A man is never alone when he can think and remember. And, surely, a soul with no joyful memories is a spirit void of love and life. I never met Mike Houston; I knew him because I admired what he wrote. One does not find it unusual to see some folks for a lifetime and never get to know them, while others he may never meet face to face but, nevertheless, come to know as intimate friends.

Houston, the Sage of the Valley, will not see his Shenandoah again. I'm grateful that he shared it with others. When we give of ourselves to that which we truly love, even death cannot finally close its doors.

It was dark as I carefully nudged my car again upon Interstate 81, to head south for home. And, remembering another writer, and another time, and another snow, I knew there would be many miles to go before I could sleep for the night.

A Nurse In Uniform

We ate lunch together in the plant cafeteria. It was the first time my oldest daughter and I had been together-just the two of us-in a long, long time. And it does seem I really got to know this charming lady by being with her awhile.

How sad that I was too busy during her early years. Back then I was involved with getting an education and doing all the dozens of other things I thought could not wait. Now, I'm old and ready to retire; and she is young and has a promising career. I saw a whole lot of a daddy in his little girl today. It is a delightful experience to hear someone express your same thoughts and goals and dreams...and, more so, from one you love so dearly.

There was a sense of excitement when she recounted the long years she has studied to acquire the knowledge that is essential to the job she will do. I'm a product of the Depression and cannot comprehend the theory that it is the responsibility of society to provide meaningful jobs. I get disturbed when I hear it said in some places that it is not important to study hard in school, or train until we are competent, and work conscientiously when we are employed. I believe among the highest calls of man is the exalted privilege of work. Success does not come by avoiding the difficult; but rather through a conquest of the impossible tasks.

The thing, I guess, that impressed me most today was the uniform my daughter wore. It represents to my way of thinking, a corps of marching humanitarians known to the sick and dying around the world. A stethoscope and other delicate instruments of her specialized vocation were carefully tucked in the smallest of pockets. Her appearance is one of high professionalism.

I sensed the noble accomplishment that is hers in wearing this nurse's badge of distinction. I remember the honor I felt when I first donned a soldier's dress. And after more than thirty years the same feeling, mixed with humility and pride, swells within me when I put it on today.

We call this esprit de corps in the Army. It is involved with a common spirit that exists among those who have an identical mission, know the same hardships and share a common danger.

It inspires enthusiasm, devotion, and a strong regard for the honor of those who wear the uniformed color. We parted, and I watched my little girl walk away. I remembered with outrageous pride her past accomplishments... from breaking a horse to painting a picture to singing. Her lyric soprano was magnificent in the Messiah but did not compare in feeling with "Sweet Little Jesus Boy," which she has sung in church since a very young girl. Her voice and that song fulfilled something deep inside me. That memory, with the sight of a neat nurse's uniform, makes this old man want to stand and cheer!

Wandering In The Valley

Among our most picturesque valleys are the Tennessee in Alabama, and the Shenandoah of the northwestern part of Virginia. Each has its own uniqueness. Virginians long ago shaved trees from their hills to provide more pasture land. This is a mark of older cultures and resembles the ancient landscapes of Europe. North Alabama, not as pressed for space and not as burdened with taxes, still has undisturbed hilltops that reflect nature as it has always been.

Our distinctive farmhouses along the Tennessee are rapidly being replaced by modern dwellings that look the same as those in towns and cities. But the countryside here in the Shenandoah is still graced with old-fashioned dwellings as lovely as those in a Grandma Moses original.

I searched today for some sign of where this artist once lived. I find as I grow older an appreciation of changing values. Not many years ago I looked for battlefields where mighty warriors fell. Now I'm wandering in the valley seeking to know more about a little farm widow who created rare and lasting beauty with the touch of talented hands.

Born Anna Mary Robertson in Washington County, New York, she began working as a hired girl at the age of twelve. After her marriage to a veteran of the Union Army, they moved to the Shenandoah and by sheer drudgery paid for their first farm. Later, having moved back to New York, Anna Mary, a widow, and too old to work in the fields, took up needlework to keep busy. Finally, because of failing eyesight, she had to abandon these "yarn pictures" and turned to painting nostalgic scenes of country life from memory. And at an age when most folk are waiting to die, she won world acclaim. Her scenes are reproduced on the best of greeting cards; her paintings are nearly priceless.

This amazing story of success that came near the end of a long and unsung life is as refreshing as the Shenandoah: It's the kind of anecdote one likes to hear, and adds a beautiful chapter to the books of art history.

Maybe within the bosom of every being there are ingredients for a grand masterpiece that could be accomplished if we but had the will of a Grandma Moses.

The Fuel Shortage

Amid predictions of extensive fuel shortages I'm reminded that in every unfortunate situation one can find something that's good, if indeed you look long and think seriously. One good that comes to my mind is the resurgence of an old American tradition-sitting around an open fireplace or a wood-burning stove on a cold evening. I think this can heal some long-nourished wounds and bind a whole lot of broken hearts and even close communication gaps between young and old.

Nostalgia left aside, I've always been an advocate of wood fires. Did you know, for instance, that a thousand gallons of fuel oil and one cord of wood each give off approximately the same amount of heat-140,000 BTU? And for the ecologist, here is another plus for wood fires: This same 1,000 gallons of oil gives off 284 pounds of harmful sulfur oxides, 5 pounds of deadly carbon monoxide, and 10 pounds of particulates (which I call soot and ashes). The cord of wood gives off more soot and ashes, 25 to 30 pounds, but less of every other kind of pollution than oil, including only 2 pounds of carbon monoxide and no sulfur oxides.

Now for the ashes-another big plus. Wood ashes are an excellent source of potash and two or three pounds broadcast per hundred square feet will give most any plant enough potash. Corn will be sweeter, tomatoes redder, carrots better, and even gladiola and dahlia roots grow bigger and healthier.

Wood ashes are also excellent insecticides for the garden. It is sort of an open secret that wood ashes heaped around the trunk of a dogwood will keep borers from digging in. We have no idea how serious the energy crisis will get before things are better. But we should prepare for the worst. I have confidence in the American system and the American people.

I believe when conditions get rough we get tough. We've survived a lot worse, from the Indians to the Great Depression. With faith in God we can meet and overcome the impossible. And I do believe the energy shortage will not be half as bad if we are sitting in front of a flickering wood fire.

Blooms And Bolls & Cotton Gins

I've always wondered why the cotton bloom was not selected as a state flower, and why the cotton boll does not appear somewhere on a state seal, and why the cotton gin is not listed as a distinctive architectural contribution to the building arts. Surely the cotton cycle-from the planted seed to the pressed bale-is as much a part of The South as the yellowhammer and the Southern pine.

There was a time when cotton really was king. It was called the money crop. Bankers and merchants anxiously awaited its maturity.  Tenants and sharecroppers depended on its power to provide a few necessary staples and to send their children to school so that they too would not have to work in the cotton fields to barely exist. And landowners used its proceeds to pay bills and taxes so cotton could be planted again another season.

All the time I was in Europe I dreamed of the time I could stand in a field and see nothing but rows and rows of cotton stalks, rather than tanks and guns and marching men. Now, when I travel to other sections of the country, it is always a wonderful welcome to return to the whitecap fields and see familiar silhouettes of cotton gins along our highways and at the crossings of the roads.

Man views these wayside fields and roadside gins in somewhat different ways. Some see through memories distorted, discolored and warped. Others look each year at the same fields, and hear the drone of the same gins, to capture a quaint beauty found nowhere else in the world.

Life, like the cotton field and the humming gin, is what we make it. Some begrudgingly work to live, while others joyously live to work. And whatever the job and wherever the task the beauty can be seen if we accept the opportunity that is ours and meet the challenge it gives.

Mother's Day

There are a lot of hills in my life. Some are rugged and rocky, others tree-shaded and serene. The most meaningful I know is the hill that holds my Mother's grave. It is an elevation of dignity and beauty. Its sublime contour is holy ground. Many years have come and gone since we placed her tired, worn body there to rest. Time, they say, heals pain. But it never does. It only touches the heavy ache with acceptance and understanding. And it provides an interim to better remember all the tender days lived with one so dear.

I'll go to that hill on Mother's Day, and walk the path that winds its way among carved stones. I shall stand beside the mound of green earth on top of that lonely height. But, all the recollections within me shall be in other places...and in our yesterdays.

I'll reminisce the old kitchen and the flower garden and the pet guineas that followed her...all lined up in a neat row. I'll taste again her pies and cakes, and feel once more her hand upon my forehead. And I'll think of the times she gave advice and of the things she'd rather I not do. I'll hear her soft voice at the front porch swing, and the hymns she played at the piano. But most of all I'll remember the sacrifices she made, and the deeds she did for those she loved. These reflections and a thousand more will tell me of Mother. But not the grave upon the hill.

Mother's love spans all time. It is the first thing learned in the cradle and does not end at the cemetery. It is a relationship especially designed and created by the One whose wisdom perceived that man cannot live by bread alone.

Getting An Early Start

I'm traveling by way of the Skyline Drive. It winds along the highest peaks and crests, and overlooks some of the most picturesque mountains and valleys in Virginia. There is a magnificence here among cliffs, hanging rocks, and tall timbers. They seem to be reaching out to touch the edge of eternity.

I read a small plaque back at Rock Fish Gap. It said there are over six hundred species of trees in this lovely rim of the Appalachians that extends from South Pennsylvania to North Georgia.

I tracked a deer across a flat mountain known locally as Big Meadows. As we faced each other in the heavy frost I was glad that I was not the hunter...and that he was not the hunted. This graceful animal bounded into the underbrush, and the chilly winds turned me back to seek the shelter of my car.

There's a rustic inn on top of Loft Mountain; from this place I can see the other side. My trip is almost over. And this is a reminder that I've reached the age when more years are behind than there are those left to go.

Maybe when we become aware of this profound knowledge it helps to explain why there have been some noticeable changes in the way we think and in the things we do. We no longer grieve over petty problems and minor disagreements.

Some things, once so important, are hardly worth all the effort and time. Big cars, expensive houses and important-sounding positions no longer leave an impression. Patience that, we once hoped for, is now within our reach. Inconveniences are not half as serious as we once believed. And we have learned...at last...to laugh at ourselves.

Another wayfarer came in to sit at the next table. He broke into my wandering thoughts to say that snow is predicted in these mountains tonight. That's exciting news. I've never met the man who would not stop to talk about weather reports. It's good to be going home. I must set my clock for the morning. I'll be getting an early start.

Our Old Hill

There's nothing difficult about being nostalgic. It comes easily. Especially when you're growing older. Somewhere within the mechanism of man there must be a gene with a built-in compass that points gently toward home. At least, more often now, I pause from time to time, and think of that hill where I came from.

It was a high plateau surrounded by a multitude of other elevations. Yet, from our home one could look down and see the valley in between. There were exciting things in that

hollow... a bubbling creek we thought much kin to the Tennessee River...a swimming hole that, in the assessment of little boys and old men, fulfilled its purpose with more splendor than the best of Olympic pools...a pasture where bare feet had carved a baseball diamond equal, in our eyes, to Yankee Stadium...and our church where Grandpa insisted that I sit straight and never slouch, always at the front and never in the back.

As I look back I see this hill and that valley as a family place. We didn't know then that all other places weren't somewhat the same. One granddad made his home with us. Our other grandparents were in Mother's old home nearby. In the flatlands below four groups of great-grandparents lived and died before my time. And in clusters there and about were aunts, uncles, and all kinds of kin. I guess it would be pleasant to say that we were reared on sacred ground.

It's fun to travel there in dreams. Often I think I hear the same whippoorwills and feel at times an invigorating freshness that comes at dawn when you awake on higher ground. I find myself measuring time and food and things as way back then. Hard work was taught as having so much virtue that even now when I know I should slow down, I can't.

Man, they say, is forever influenced by his environment. The ways we think and do, even the ways we pronounce our words, are affected by those early formative years. I can't go back to that hill. But as all things of a true and lasting value, my hill somehow finds its way back to me.

Impressions

Several years ago I attended the Department of Defense Seminar for an update on research and development. One demonstration amazed me more than all the other fantastic breakthroughs in modern warfare technology. Photographs were made of men who were no longer present and of machines after they had been removed. These supersensitive cameras captured impressions left behind through slight variations in heat that affected light.

They told us that the law of impression is as much a science as the law of gravity. Impression is a form of energy, and like other forms of energy, it can be transposed and transferred, but never destroyed.

Carbon 14, a heavy radioactive isotope used in tracer studies and in dating archaeological and geological materials of thousands and millions of years ago, is another successful extension of this science of impression.

Things may die or cease to be but the impressions made by their existence cannot be lost. The earth and the air about us serve as vast libraries. Man may someday develop the device that will enable him to unlock secret chambers and know again the fragrance of the ancient rose that grew in Solomon's garden and to hear once more the voice of the prophets in the old Judean hills.

I cannot comprehend the technology of this science, but the theory is the same that I learned as a child. Man is slowly discovering the mechanics of a theology taught by the sages and prophets from the beginning. There is a Book of Life, and in it is recorded our every word, and thought, and deed.

One Beautiful Day

Though we put forth our best efforts, our blunders cause silent moans and sometimes secret wishes for the earth to open and swallow our absurdities. Yet, such are always self-inflicted attitudes for defeat. They spoil and bring to ruin the best of men. To remember things forgiven yesterday is old nonsense. They rob a new day of its hopes and challenges that make for life's grand adventures.

Years ago, while counting what seemed endless days of confinement in the hospital, I learned that the best way is to live one day at a time. Each new day is a rare gift, more valuable than all the treasures of the world combined. Someone said that today is the first day of the rest of your life.

"Write it on your heart that every day is the best day of the year." A lot of frets and anxieties are invasions from yesterdays. And as Attila, king of the Huns, they plague and plunder to deprive and bring despair. The richest folk I know live in sunny rooms where there is light among even dark shadows of tears and heavy loads. They really own their day. They neither sell it to little people who thrive to argue, nor lease it to petty annoyances and remembrances of past disappointments.

No man and no thing should ever be big enough to cause the ruin of one beautiful day.

April And Showers

Long ago a lyric was written-a glamorous, haunting song called "April in Paris." It has probably influenced many travelers to buy airline tickets to try to capture the romance of April in the most beautiful city in the world. Actually, they find rain, cold wind to the bone and sometimes snow. I was there; Paris is much nicer later in the year.

While in Venice, Robert Browning penned, "Oh, to be in England, now that April's here..." while thinking of his homeland. Not only are France and England uncomfortable in April; our own continent experiences twisting winds and rivers of rain.

But so what if the sky is cloudy and violent...there are days of sunshine when the flags straighten up after the rain and the roses are full and violets cover the woods.

The Latin name for April means "to open." It fits well this month when the whole world begins to open to warm and gracious summer.

Airways And Highways

I never cease to marvel at man's ability to fly...to cruise above the clouds...to turn weary and long days of highway travel into short hours of comfort and expediency. There is a certain feeling of being aloft...away from the familiar...viewing earth from horizon to horizon...seeing the smallness of things... knowing a little more the perspective relationship of our own world to the billions of other planets in far-flung galaxies. How much greater this reveals the omnipotent hand of the one who created and controls complex ways of life.

Yet, with all its luxury and inspiration, the airway, to my way of thinking, cannot compare with a highway. No matter how slow the journey, time is not wasted when we really see the tall tree...the wayside goldenrod...feet the simple atmosphere of hamlets, towns and cities.

I like to soak up every mile that winds through valleys, climbs mountains, and crosses rivers. Every bend in the road awakens a desire to know what is ahead. I never see a mountain without wanting to go to the other side. Every river and lake tempts me to see the far shore.

Woods and fields, holding the land's growing things, blend each passing mile into a travel-log of adventure. The skyscraper... the rustic fence...the mansion...and the shanty afford a surreptitious peer into the ways that man, endowed with dominion, has worked to sometimes succeed...and often fail.

Travel, if you will, by hops and skips, or one straight jaunt, on plane across the land. But I'll wait for another time. I must know things not yet seen...fill blank pages in my journal with all the treasures highways give. Maybe when it is filled...all notations complete...and its covers frayed and yellowed with age, then I'll join you in flights beyond the horizon.

Meanwhile, I'll keep my appointment along roads that slowly unwind to reveal all the various aspects of our land.

The Fourth Of July

The Fourth of July is a lot of things to a lot of people. Barbecue will be cooked, hand cranks on the ice cream freezer will be turned, cold watermelons will be cut, and picnics and outings with family and friends will be enjoyed.

It will be a full day at our place. Our celebration begins by

ringing the old farm bell to arouse a sleeping family. By breakfast time we are in the woods below the house. The aroma of coffee, bacon and eggs cooking in crisp morning air is for us, the best of the Fourth!

But this holiday is more than these things. It is our day to honor a majestic land and the best form of government on earth. No state and no system of society in all history of nations can begin to measure that which we have.

It is sometimes easy to take for granted our heritage and our blessings. One of the dangers of affluence and greatness is apathy and ingratitude. Freedom is never free. Its cost is so high that only those willing to give of themselves can truly know its privileges. And the price of democracy is never paid in full.

The story of the struggle of man to establish a form of government of the people and by the people is one of the heartbreaks of history. Time and again determined efforts were crushed by despots and invading hordes. And not until the Declaration of Independence by the brave and courageous souls of the thirteen colonies was it attained to survive. There has never been anything to compare with these United States in the dignity and devotion and destiny of its people.

The will to remain free is our sacred trust and awesome responsibility. And to renew our faith in democracy is our highest call on Independence Day.

> *Each generation must carry its load and earn the right to remain free.*

The Winds Of Life

One of the haunting things about the West is the summer wind. It blows continuously across the prairies and deserts. No matter how hot the sun, the wind is there to cool in the shade of evening. This wind seems as ageless as the sand and the rocks and the mesas. It is not an occasional gust to bend the lonely mesquite and almost sway the cactus. It comes from nowhere and goes nowhere and is everywhere.

Ancient man must have stood amazed in its brutal strength. And generations to be born will yet be awed by its mighty presence. Timelessly the summer winds batter these thousands of miles of our flat lands in the West.

One evening I sat in the shade of our camp near Kingman, Arizona, and watched some people attempt to pitch their tent. They fought the resolute winds until night fell. And, finally, in defeat, picked up their canvas and left. Theirs must have been a sleepless night. But I was sure they were not the first nor the last to lose in the battle against this onslaught of power found in the winds on the plains.

I thought how much our life is like this. It is good to rest in the shade of trees, but real life makes no permanent provision for this sheltered reprieve. Better to be remembered for having tried to win against the winds of time. We may lose, but let it be said we tried.

Being Alone

Sometimes the travels get weary, and the body tired, and the mind exhausted. It is then we need a place for meditation, alone and apart from the busy and complicated activities that push and pull us until we nearly break.

I'm aware that many fear the melancholy experience when separated from people. Yet, the longer I live the more convinced I am that those who find no place for solitude are poorer than those who have learned the art of being alone.

You don't have to be too selective to find a retreat; beside a stream or in the far corner of the garden will do. And how blessed we are to live among plentiful and peaceful hills yet uninhabited by man. I think these isolated heights are the best of sanctuaries. They capture the deep meaning of a beautiful thought from the most ancient of literature: "I will lift up mine eyes unto the hills, from whence cometh my help."

Henry David Thoreau once said, "The mass of men lead lives of quiet desperation." He also said, "I went to the woods because I wished to see if I could not learn what life had to teach, and not, when I came to die, discover that I had not lived."

Even though we are destined to know problems and anxieties all through the journey of life, it is good when we can withdraw into the lofty woods of our mind and rest within the solitude of silence. This is a balm that heals and renews.

The Creator designed great cathedrals of hills and trees to use in our times of private despair. We may die a little. But there is alchemy in the solitude of the soul, alone, and yet surrounded with the presence of windy trees...mossy rocks...gentle waters...and the One who understands.

His Orange Dream

My friend looked rather awkward with gangling legs a stride a bicycle, going here and there. He was lonely after his wife died, had no living relatives, and, too, was a newcomer to our town.

He gained distinction locally. Saw an abandoned corner filled with weeds and leaves. Took upon himself to cultivate it with flowers and shrubs of every sort. One could find him there almost every day in the Spring and Summer with a hoe in his hand. It wasn't a formal garden, never one to blend in with Georgetown or Williamsburg, or even Wilson Park. Fact is, there was nothing artistic about it. But that was another of his simple ways with life. He merely heaped up beds and planted flowers and they grew and bloomed.

And the vacant lot became beautiful because he cared and loved and worked to raise flowers where once it was ugly, unkept and neglected. Occasionally a reporter would take a picture and write a story about his hobby.   So, he acquired sort of a Johnny Appleseed legend.

He was interesting because he liked people and flowers and was unselfish and gave of himself to others. I think these are marks of a truly great man.

One night in his hospital room, as we talked, I watched as he meticulously peeled an orange as if preparing a stated dinner. Carefully he sectioned the fruit and laid each piece in a neat row on a stand beside his bed.

I wondered. Then he told me of his dream the night before about eating a delicious orange. Said he woke in the dark hours hungry for one. "Tonight," he said, "when I wake these will be here ready to eat."

We said our prayer and I left to learn next day that my friend died before dawn. I've been quite curious since to know if he fulfilled his dream before he went away. But it really doesn't matter.

Knowing his faith and appreciation of the beautiful, I somehow suspect he is busy with his hoe in the Eternal City raising flowers and shrubs and maybe cultivating a tree that will grow big, ripe oranges.

I'm no theologian, but I cannot believe that Heaven can be less than a continuation of our labors of love.

Grandmothers And Medicine

I've thought a lot about the therapeutic and theological roles played by grandmothers in my far-off yesterdays. They had the best soothing salve a boy could find when he skinned his knee. Their answer was dependable when he came out with his childhood questions about God and how things came to be.

And, somehow, these patient little ladies possessed mystical powers that could calm fears during the worst of storms and in the blackest of nights. Surely, a child's chance in a big and complex world is not helped when he has to face it during his first years without the tender assistance of a grandmother's care.

My grandma easily could have been a character in a Norman Rockwell painting. She looked and lived her part well. She had the kind of Victorian virtue that someway got handed out to little Southern ladies in her day. And Grandma knew the Bible better than a faculty or seminary professors. Her wisdom surely matched the ancient sages. She had an uncanny sixth sense. And seemed to know something was going to happen long before it did. She could tell spellbinding stories. And, when least expected, would inject a funny yarn, all mixed up with a mischievous sparkle in her eyes.

Mama-that's what we grandchildren called her-lived a quiet and unassuming life. She died slowly and in pain, but to the end was serene and confident in the faith she had known all her days. Grandmother had taught us to live to die. She said that death was as natural as life, and warned that he who was afraid to die was surely afraid to live.

Today I see alarming statistics about problem children, and read about specialized training they need when they become disturbed. It is then I go back in time and think about Mama, and give thanks for all she gave us.

I suspect that at least half of a child's sensitive problems would not have been if full advantage had been made of our world's most effective human resource...the old-fashioned and ever-kindly grandmother; for she is the grandest and most professional medicine of all.

Vicki

It was said she was an invalid in body. Yet, her strength was more powerful than an army of marching men. I came as her teacher and became a learner. I learned of compassion rarely seen. I saw love in the purest form. Its depth in beauty was more refreshing than a mountain spring. It flowed from her bedside to the family, to the church, to the community, and among strangers who chanced to pass by.

I have reflected many hours upon the meaning of her life and this death. As most men are, so am I, limited by what we sense and see and hear. And I had a feeling from the beginning that she was a revelation. And through her I learned more about the love and goodness of God than from a hundred books and a hundred sermons.

Life is a mystery. The unseen holds even greater miracles-had we the eyes to see. And I suspect that every generation or so our Father sends a special life to open blinded eyes. We knew about love. But we were too hurried to know its reality. We needed a teacher.

And this child came with that message. And she personified love at its best. How often we disappoint God by our inadequacies and half-hearted efforts and failures. But this special gift did not fail. Faithfully and perfectly she fulfilled her mission and our dimmed eyes were opened and we saw love, not in words, but in deed, and in truth.

This was not an ordinary life and not really a death. This child was a blessing unaware, an angel in disguise. And at last we understand what Paul meant when he wrote: "...for thereby some have entertained angels unawares."

Four More Months

I sometimes wonder what value we place on a day, a week, a month, or a year. If we are in good health, chances are we give little thought to these measures of unsearchable riches. I remember reading how Queen Elizabeth cried out in anguish at her hour of death that she would give her kingdom for one more day.

In my graduate studies in economics I learned a new term- incommensurable intangible. Somehow, it sticks with me with a lot of thoughts. When a field commander assesses his plans and options before a battle, there are things he can place a value upon, such as tanks, guns, supplies. But, then, he must decide what risks he is willing to take in the loss of his own men. This is what our Army calls an incommensurable intangible. There is no measurable formula for this kind of appraisal. And, in my way of thinking, this is true as we value our days.

Last week I went by the Nursing Home. Buddy is one patient I try to spend some time with. He has been invalid as long as I've known him. I never asked, but suspect he was born that way. His body is twisted and bent, his legs crippled and weak, and his speech slow and impaired. But Buddy's mind is as sharp as a razor's edge, and his humor as jolly as a chuckle, and his faith as solid as Job's.

He talks a lot about life. His appreciation of what little is his shows through in the way he thinks and the things he does. He has a genuine concern for the problems and feelings of others. And this is the mark of a real gentleman. Yet, he rarely mentions the excruciating pains that afflict his days and nights. And this is hard to understand.

He is confined most of the time to his bed. But on this last visit I found him sitting lonely and alone in a wheelchair. Tubes ran from his frail body to a nearby apparatus. His doctor had just told him had maybe four months to live.

I stumbled and blundered and tried as best I could to think of a comforting word. The best I could offer was, well, maybe this could be good news. Then was when Buddy raised his face from the side of his chair. Looking now with renewed expectancy and hope he said, "The only thing I fear, Mac, is that it may be longer than four months." I went away to ask forgiveness for the way I misuse my days.

To Our First Granddaughter

Your birthday will be a day we will remember. Your arrival into our family was precisely when a full moon was at its zenith. The earth, bathed by a shower only hours before, was fresh and pure. How appropriate for this occasion of your birth.

Our prayers began months before you came. And we were grateful and knew the goodness of our Father's love when we heard your first cry and saw your alert countenance as you looked the first time into this dazzling immensity of earth with its challenge so vast and majestic to the soul's intellect.

When I saw my lovely granddaughter this night, I had no fear for her future. What a tremendous ad-vantage to begin life in the morning hours of a space age.

My Dear One, I know you shall face the to-morrows of life with confidence that there is a power that guides every trusting path. I wish for you a courage that shall not be shaken, and hope that your love will know no barrier, and believe that your faith will be strong enough for the shadows that inevitably fall upon the wall of every room.

And I pray that God will use you as He wills.
- Your Grandpa

Gift Of A Hat

He was a lonely old man confined in his last years to a nursing home. His children were scattered. He seemed to enjoy my visits and our prayers together; I suppose this was one of his few contacts with the outside world. I learned a lot about him. He loved the church and was a leader in his congregation for over sixty years, until they put him away to die. But there was one conflict. This bothered me.

And I wanted to do something about it. His oldest boy went into the far country of trouble long ago; and after years of grief and disappointment, the old fellow had turned from his son. There had been no contacts, no visits, no letters. I thought it time for the prodigal son to come home.

After many talks and much persuasion the son, obviously aged by a hard life, went with me, and together we entered the room to see the one he had tried to forget. Their meeting was formal and awkward and stilted. And I was disappointed. Maybe it was too much to hope for after all these passing years.

I had failed in bringing them together. But as we were leaving a strange thing happened; the old man looked at his son and said, "I'd love to have your hat." The son removed his hat and handed it to the old man, who carefully examined the gift and looked again at his son. I saw tears. So did the prodigal son as he bent over and took his father in his arms.

The frost of too many years melted and there was a genuine reunion. Sometimes it takes more love to receive than to give. Love is a gift of God. It moves in mysterious ways.

Granny's Mountain

Grandma loved her mountain. She had no legal title to this lofty height. It was hers by right of love. No power on earth can take away this claim of her heart. In fact, love is the only perfect title through which we can posses and hold eternity. She has been gone more than two decades, but it will always be my Granny's mountain.

When cares and pressures of the world close in about me, it becomes my fortress against pain and despair, and my sally port into visions of a more beautiful day.

In need of retreat the other day I drove across the majestic crest of this isolated place and looked over the vast valley below. I wandered through deep woods and found ancient bloodroots and sweet Williams and tiny bluebells, evidences of a glorious spring and reminders that some things remain the same. I stood transfixed in the magic of God's own design.

Some only see the ornamental in mighty monuments and volumes of steel and concrete, but the rarest of all beauty is in dainty and delicate proportions of nature's sculpture. Grandma must have gathered these wild flowers in her youth. But, I found them too sacred to despoil, and carried away only the remembrance of loveliness to refresh my soul.

Granny left her mountain when a young girl and never returned except in dreams and memories and in the stories she often told her children's children. In the long ago when I was young and Grandmother was in the winter of life, we planned a special journey to this mountain of nostalgia. But as the day approached, she shook her head and said she couldn't go home again. It would not be the same and one couldn't risk destroying cherished dreams. Maybe now I understand.

But I'm thankful I can go to her mountain. I'm glad God made the high places along with vales and coastal plains. We live and serve in the valleys and beside the seas of human needs, and visit mountain peaks to refresh and revive our tired spirits. How dull and drab life would be if there were no Granny's mountains to climb, or no delicate charm of God's art to behold. For such builds man's strength and increases his faith as he strives to serve among people in the valley below.

The Garden Hoe

There has been a revolutionary change in working with a hoe since my boyhood days. In fact, the longer I think about it, the more I recognize and appreciate the transformation. For the change has not been in the hoe, but in me.

The simple device is used to clean out weeds, grass, and all the undesirables from the rows and to thin growing plants and keep the soil loose. Artifacts from primitive peoples show its basic structure is the same today as in the beginning. It always had a long handle with a sharp instrument at the end. I guess there is no way to improve the design. There have been attempts with modernizations. But machinery, like the roto-tiller and such, can never replace the effect of hoeing with this common old garden tool.

In my youth I loathed the thought of this hard chore. I remembered advice from an old-timer in the field who said, "If you're gonna' make a mark in this world, son, don't let it be with a hoe." And dreamed of the day when I could lay it down and never use it again.

But I've never gotten far from the hoe. And now that my hair is slowly fading to gray, I long for opportunities to be alone with my hoe...and know its source of therapy for a weary soul. I find I now love that which once I loathed.

Hard work with dirt-soiled hands can solve a hundred problems. Man can become exhausted enough to thoroughly enjoy a time for rest. I think that I have not found any relaxation as satisfying as leaning leisurely against the handle of the hoe in the shade by the garden's edge.

When I retire from all the harassments and complexities of my many activities in life, I can think of nothing better for my remaining days than to enjoy the sweat that comes by working with the hoe. And when, at last, I'm called to come through the door, if it's all the same with my Maker, I'd be mighty pleased to go with the hoe in my hand.

Papa Hall

He went home last Sunday. That's a good time for a preacher to take his leave. Throughout most of his life he was busy with last-minute sermon preparations, at this time of the week. He left all this behind for younger preachers to do. His work here was over. He needed his rest.

Our family will miss this sage of the home and pulpit. We'll treasure those moments of laughter he gave us, and those unbelievable looks of amazement on the faces of the great-grandchildren when Papa would complete his dinner and dance across the room. They could never accept the fact that he was an old man. Even our animals received a share of his teasing. We still talk about the time we looked out the window to see Papa down on all fours chasing the calf over the barn lot.

But when Papa prayed he was sincere and earnest. And when he stood behind the pulpits of the great churches of our conference he was the personification of dignity and warmth and love. We shall long treasure the memory of his rich tenor voice proclaiming in his own special way the great truths of the Christ he loved and served.

He lived a full life. He had a religion of joy and excitement and love and it was solid and strong, and he was dedicated and faithful. I was glad when the soloist sang "He Lives" at the funeral. This was Papa's victorious hymn. Those words of Easter morning were his great truth and fact. The Lord lives. He lives, we know that we who loved him have not lost him. This grand preacher will live forever.

Sopping Molasses

Not everybody knows how to enjoy molasses. Most folks live a lifetime and never learn the fine art of sopping. And sopping is the only way to get the very best from the syrup. First you pour a small amount of red-eye gravy in your plate and cover it all over with thick sorghum. Then break a biscuit in half, hold it firmly, and mix the sorghum and hot gravy by running the biscuit criss-cross and then round and round. When you get this far it's just ripe for sopping. You can do this several ways, but the best method I follow is to twist what's left of the biscuit between your thumb and forefinger and make a scoop. And the bigger the biscuit the more you can scoop and the more you can scoop the better the sopping.

Now, I've found that this doesn't go over too well in certain places. I confess, I never did know what to do with the ham gravy they serve in some of these sophisticated restaurants. I usually just leave it in the bowl-for want of a jar of sorghum and a buttermilk biscuit.

It is sorghum time again and I have been wondering about our lives and the way we have lost the simple ways to a more complicated and modern way of living. We worry too much, regret too often, join too many clubs, and run in too many directions. All along the way we collect the clutter of worthless and ungainful things while the really good and worthwhile we could pursue pass us by.

With sorghum I can't do much in decorated settings of china, silver and crystal. Just give me a plain plate and plenty of room. It may not show the best etiquette, but believe me, there is a whole lot of joy in such a meal!

Firewood And Folk

I've sat about many firesides. Have watched lots of log fires. Some flames leap and glow and quickly expire. Others burn low and long and leave embers to blaze again on another day. No two sticks are alike, and no two trees give the same volume of heat. Resinous softwoods, like pine, spruce, and fir, flare up rapidly and give out invigorating warmth, but left alone will quickly burn out. This is convenient if you want a quick source of heat and are afraid to leave a glowing log when the evening is over.

Now for a dependable and long-lasting fire, heavier hardwoods such as ash, beech, birch, maple, and oak are the best. Of these, the oak gives the most uniform, short flames, and produces steady, glowing ashes.

There used to be a lot of firewood connoisseurs in this part of the country. Still some around now, but the best I have known over other years are gone. They selected wood for the fireplace as carefully as the Belgians I knew in the long ago chose their rare cheese. Each tender of the family hearth had his own special formula, picked his wood carefully, and weighed his needs and tastes before building his fire.

The heat that a fireplace produces depends upon the concentration of woody material, resin, water and ash contents of each log. Since woods are of different compositions, they ignite at various temperatures and give off a variable range of heat value. For this reason, achieving the ideal fire requires a mixture of light and heavy woods.

And though not recommended by most old-timers, from whom it has been my privilege to learn, I still like to mix a few sticks of green along with the seasoned. This gives a sizzling sound that adds a note of cheer to a cold, damp night.

A nostalgic effect can also be achieved by adding woods of fruit trees such as apple and cherry and from nut trees such as beech, hickory and pecan. The smoke from these logs generally resembles the fragrance of the fruit. Too, these are steady flame producers, although they do not have the greater heating values of the oak.

In all my years of gazing into a fireplace I never cease to compare firewood to folk. Logs, like people, are different and useful in their individual and peculiar ways. Yet they serve a higher and nobler cause when combined to cooperate and blend together their many talents as one.

Apple Blossom Time

Blooming apple trees in any part of the country are the essence of beauty. And never more so than around and about our own home. Nostalgia affects most of us at special times during the year. Surely, wherever the gentle man may go, his thoughts must look toward home at apple blossom time. I think I would not want to miss these few days...not for all the tourist sites in the whole world!

There are several apple trees on our place. The favorite and most highly prized shades the front walk. It is not of a brand name variety...just a yellow, old-fashioned horse apple. Bushels of the fruit cover the ground every summer, even when early frost withers the foliage. It is always reliable.

It is a major chore to keep the yard clean...and sort out the ripe, the too-ripe, and the rotten. While working at this task last year, Lindsey, our granddaughter, ran up with her paper bag to assist. After awhile, seeing how tired I was, and wishing to call

attention to the help being given, the very young and tiny girl said, "Granddaddy, I'm your little apple-sacker."

Some day my "little apple-sacker" will know and appreciate a certain bit of knowledge about this tree. It was tenderly rooted, watched over, and cared for by her great-grandfather. It was far more than a fruit tree with him. Its early, fragile shoot came from the last gnarled survivor of his father's orchard. Apprehensive that his children and grandchildren could not enjoy its flowers in the Spring and its steaming pies in the summer, he determined to perpetuate the seed.

Time and again he tried and failed and succeeded only at his final chance. The old stump had rotted and fallen to the ground.

This was a labor of love. For he who had planted was not to live to see the radiant grandeur of its first spring. I look at the pale pink blooms each spring and think of the values we give to life. Surely here is one of a grandfather's lasting rewards...When he lives and labors so that other generations can know a little more of the beauty of the earth.

The Name Plate

Life on this earth has a purpose for every being. Every existence, no matter how brief, has a definite and responsible mission. I believe man comes to weave into life's fabric a quality that will live when his presence long has faded into time. If with God's help we try, there can be no final failure in those things that are eternal.

I pondered these thoughts at the retirement party for Miss Stella Winegart. She came to work for the Army in 1943, and for half of her life has shuffled in and out of a city of 30,000 workers in one tremendous building called the Pentagon.

I have worked with Stella these past years during my annual assignments with the Army. Yet, knew little about her, other than she seemed efficient and sat behind a desk which had a large name plate in bold letters that told who she was. I knew, too, that Miss Winegart had weathered many storms and crises in this nerve center of our armed forces, and she looked tired and old beyond her years.

On the day of the party our staff gathered about her desk. A plain white cake was cut into many little pieces and served with small cups of flat-flavored punch. The General read what sounded like a canned speech in appreciation of her long years of dedicated work.

We all wished her farewell, and there were a few remarks about how she would be missed. Then, the frail old lady picked up her few personal belongings, and I watched as she turned the corner in the long corridor that led somewhere outside to a place we have come to know as retirement.

Early next morning I watched the janitor clean up what was left of the party, and, seemingly, as a final gesture, he picked up the name plate with the bold letters that spelled her name and tossed it into the trash can.

Somehow, this becomes a haunting message when we think upon the ways we actually spend our days and years. God forbid that all we do in this life will someday end and we'll leave behind nothing of lasting value.

The Healing Of Blinded Eyes

I was prejudiced. And my only excuse is that I was too young and knew so little. Yet, that long-ago regret still serves as a reminder that real friends come from all walks of life. We were leaving Europe behind on the U.S.S. J.W. McAndrews. Most of us had been together a long time. Trials and Hardships over there gave us a certain bond of lasting fellowship. Others joined our unit at the port. One fellow, among these newcomers, was a alcoholic. And I did not conceal my dislike. He gave no trouble; but I was determined to make life hard for him.

Responsible for keeping our area of the ship clean and orderly, I made sure he did more than his share of the hardest work. I thought it would teach him a lesson. But I was to be the learner.

Our ship landed at New York and we were to hurriedly march, with heavy packs on our backs, up a steep back to the waiting train. But I stumbled and groped helplessly about. A cinder had blinded my eye with intense pain. I needed my friends but they had passes me by. It was every man for himself in an atmosphere filled with excitement as all scrambled for home.

A forsaken feeling numbed my senses almost as much as the pain. Then, in unbelief, I felt the gentle touch of a comforting hand. He lifted my heavy packs to place them upon his already burdened back, and guided me safely to the train and found for me a seat to rest. And with skill and patience he removed the cinder from my swollen eye.

At last I could see. And I saw that the good Samaritan who came to my rescue was the drunk who had endured my blinded prejudice. This old soldier, afflicted with a crippling weakness, had a heart more compassionate that I to this day have acquired. My detrimental dislike of this weakness in others was replaced that day with a tender feeling. They, too, need a helping hand. And I learned there is good in every man. Some are strong and some are weak, but all are made in the image of the Shepherd who taught that we should love our neighbor even as we love ourselves.

"Auld Lang Syne" Or "Old Long Ago"

Poets long have penned sad eulogies to old years in passing. One of the best New Year's Eve traditions is sing the Scotland ballad, "Auld Lang Syne," or 'Old Long Ago." There's a sweet sentiment in remembering good events, favorite places, and special friends. Yet, another dimension is added to this nostalgia when the passing of time erases even old landmarks once known so fondly.

Bulldozers rush in to level ancient hills. They fill our ponds and cover secluded marshes where wild ferns grow. And destroy a part of us in the process.

Tangled woods that beckoned a growing boy are now a sea of black asphalt, constantly reaching out in tidal waves to claim more of memories' receding shorelines. I once thought this would be the last citadel of my youth, and surely must remain forever the same. I was wrong. And they are no more.

Familiar voices are strangely silent now. We are stronger because they gave so much unselfishness in our yesterdays. They are gone. We are alone. And it cannot be the same.

Sooner or later all things change, old fortresses fall, and the only calendars of ending years are those that live in the colorful pictures painted within our soul.

The passing of each old year is an era never to be regained. But it need not die. We can satisfy our hunger for its lingering touch by a memory brimming with life and sound and things warming to the eye and heart. A wonderful part of mans existence is in the past. And though tomorrow we will face hardship, and know our portion of trial, and feel again the bitter pain of battle, these will be easier when old days are added to new in a grand ceremony of simple truth and unselfconscious beauty.

For I reckon that our memories are the beginnings of our eternity. And old years are never lost we added to our yesterdays.

Digging Potatoes

I've been thinking about the plain, unadorned, ordinary potato. Next to wheat, corn, and rice, this tasty vegetable is man's most valuable source of food. Cultivated originally by Indians in South America, the tuber was introduced into North America and Europe in the sixteenth century. Its smooth, leafless underground stems-differing from the fine and fibrous roots-produce the staple that graces our tables in so many appetizing ways.

My granddaughter and I dug our crop today. We didn't get many, but we had a delightful time. She said it was like finding Easter eggs. Our knees, hands, and clothes were covered with dirt. How else would an old man and a little girl go about such a weighty task?

I think it is important to dig about in the earth. In fact, there are few jobs associated with the farm where a man can work and not get dirty. Poor is he who has never worn a pair of overalls stained with the faithful hues of sweat and soil. For he has missed the grand adventure of delving into the chemicals of creation.

A fellow can grow weary and exhausted in the potato patch. But it's a physical tiredness...the kind that contributes to sleep that leads to rest...and gives a sense of accomplishment which adds to one's spiritual dimension. Mental fatigue affects the condition of emotion, and sometimes causes a break under the stress. But physical weariness from labor in the soil can become a therapy to the mind and soul.

I've heard one or two honors along life's way, and many adventures exciting to recall. But there will be few events treasured more highly than digging potatoes and watching a little girl's face laugh in delight with each turn of the plow that brought so many surprises from beneath the earth.

Somehow, in the long life of experience, things small and common add more to the measure of life than the greater events. And these are the gifts of pleasure we love to remember.

Father's Day

Father's Day has found its own place on our calendar. I'm always appreciative of the opportunity to honor the captain who steered our ship through the early shallows and made sure we were prepared for the deep waters and rough voyages ahead. My gentle Dad earned affection and esteem from a big family.

As I look back now I know something of the sacrifice he made. I'm glad he believed in putting first things first. Father's Day sometimes causes a few of us who fill that role to pause and reflect upon how we meet our task. The boy and girl business makes up the most awesome of all responsibilities placed upon the shoulders of parents. In this work we have only one chance. If we fail, there is no way of erasing the mistake... no starting over again...no consolation in thinking next time we'll do better.

My daughters are grown now. I'm proud of them. But I missed so much of their youth. Yesterday they needed companionship in a thousand ways. I was too busy at the task of making a living, mending fences, caring for other people's problems and doing chores I thought could not wait.

I would change a few things if allowed to live my life again. I'd say no to other people...I'd resist outside pressures... I'd put off a lot of work that could wait. I'd put first things first. I would reach for and hold on to every valuable moment... and talk with little girls about childhood things...and play with them...and be there to read stories at bedtime.

But it's too late now. Time does not wait for the busy man. Each Father's Day I wish that somehow I could recapture some of those years that went by so fast. I would give my daughters all the time that little girls need. I'd put first things first. And I'd really try to be the best daddy in all the world.

The Bear, The Hat, & The Sugar Bowl

The Sugar Bowl Game in the newly constructed indoor stadium one New Year's Eve was a tremendous victory for Alabama and the South. A lot of people will remember those two long passes for a lot of years. And we in the Tennessee Valley can be mighty proud of our own Ozzie Newsome.

Yet the thing that impressed me most had nothing to do with the game...or the bands...or the crowd. Coach Bear Bryant came onto a field hatless for the first time that anybody could remember. When asked about it, he said something about how his Arkansas mother had taught him not to wear a hat indoors.

Regardless of the fads that come and go...this will always be one of the true marks of a real gentleman. Recently, while waiting with other patients in a medical office, an old-timer came in with his hat on and sat down beside his wife. With all the charm of a beautiful lady, she whispered, "Is the roof leaking?" And, catching her gentle suggestion, he removed his hat...with some embarrassment...then looked around to see if others had noticed.

I thought of her when the Bear displayed the courage of a great heritage associated with noble people. And as the Bear gave credit for his well-mannered and admirable behavior to his mother of long ago...I suspect that for every polished and courteous man...that somewhere in his life there is a gentle and elegant mother...sister...wife...daughter. Refined, cultured and graceful ladies are as roses in early spring. How poor the world and we men would be without them.

The Enchanted Forest

A child's world is magic and full of exciting make-believe things. And yet it is real and filled with a measure of love so trusting that grownups can hardly seem to fathom it at all. My grandson and I have our own special place that nobody else could possibly understand. Trees have names and grass clumps are fairy houses and animals are almost like people.

Piedmont the Owl lives at the top of an ageless oak almost hidden at the north side of our farm. Pokie Turtle is in the shallow part of the ditch near the old fence row on the west boundary.

Cheery Chipmunk lives in the cool shade of the mulberry grove, and Tweetie Bird's nest is almost hidden among the leaves in the fence row hedge. Timothy Squirrel, Slick Fox, Jay Weasel, Fluffy Rabbit, Howard Hawk, and Ellis the

Bumblebee are the other characters in our wide circle of critter friends.

This little two-year-old boy sits alertly upon my lap and we drive the tractor to all these well-hidden nooks about the place. He is bewitched not only by what is seen and heard, but also by the unseen and unheard. I think for him that time surely seems to stand still.

I can tell you that it's easy to be a grandfather. All you have to do is to turn back the years to memories of long ago when for you there was, too, a wonderland filled with all the mysteries of a little boy's delights.

Someday my little grandson will outgrow his grandpa's country. Then the giant called time will not remain immobile. Problems and burdens of the adult world will fit squarely upon his shoulders.

And when his world is crowded with the cares that put gray in men's hair, maybe he will find the path to our enchanted forest to grasp again the unseen and hear again the voices from a little boy's yesterday.

Billowing Clouds

As I write, United Airlines Flight 596 is cruising at the altitude of 34,000 feet. From a window seat I see only blankets of clouds below. All the earth is hidden beyond a gulf through which eyes cannot see. But there is a green earth beyond... where people live, flowers bloom, and streams flow into mighty rivers.

For company on this trip I brought along professor Bronowski's work, The Ascent of Man. This is a tremendous account of man and the civilization he has built with power through knowledge. The dramatic series of events and discoveries throughout the history of time came by those who could look beyond a curtain that separates the seen from the unseen.

Man has gained so small a fragment of this vast reservoir of knowledge. The truly wise are humbled by the poverty of their education. Yet, the human race has always been retarded by those who are armed with ignorance and dictatorial with dogma.

I've reached the age described ingloriously as the declining years. I do not accept this. But if it is true, I would wish to proclaim that this wonderful life has been a grand adventure... and that I shall continue to enjoy the coming of each new day and all the discoveries it brings.

Death does not loom as fear, but rather as another trip on the final and uncancellable flight. The runway will not be approached with apprehension, but rather with exciting anticipation of seeing at last the mountains and valleys and refreshing waters beyond other horizons now concealed by these billowing clouds.

Visiting A Bison Farm

I knew someday I would visit this unusual farm in the Shenandoah. So, last night I stayed at a quaint inn in Harrisonburg. This morning I feasted on the best of sugar-cured ham. And, before noon, drove to this lovely part of the valley where wild buffalo live.

I learned a lot from the manager of the ranch. For instance, a fellow can't outrun a buffalo. These animals are capable of charging at lethal speeds of thirty miles an hour. You must never turn your back on one, and the safest way to handle a bison is to stay out of its way.

A hybrid animal called "beefalo', can be produced with a bison cow and a bovine bull, but never with a bison bull and a bovine cow. These strange-looking offspring cannot be classified as new species because they cannot reproduce themselves. But they are becoming a profitable item on the marketplace in the form of steaks, roasts, and even beef-a-lo-burgers.

But that gem of knowledge most interesting was that the American buffalo has stubbornly resisted domestication since first observed by the early white man. The bison is one of earth's rare and tame-less creatures.

Domestication of animals was the keystone of early civilization. This brought about a transition from nomadic life to farming. The hearthstone of man's first permanent home could not have been established without the power of the draft animal.

Comparison of the old world and the new at the time of Columbus is summed up by the observation that the Indians were lacking in the draft power of domesticated animals. The dog, they say, was the first to live with man. Then came the goat and sheep. Taming of the horse brought not only rapid movement and adventure, but the concept of modern warfare as well.

The armored tank and the jet fighter are but adaptations of the fearless warrior on his steed. It is written that of all that man has accomplished, nothing has given him more self-esteem and personal satisfaction than owning a horse. Historically, this animal was the chief source of transportation from about 2000 B.C. to some sixty or seventy years ago. And that's a record not soon to be broken. Steam locomotion came and went in less than a century. And the gasoline engine is now faced with dwindling sources of energy.

An old saying hints that the battle was lost for the want of a horse. I suppose it could be suggested that the buffalo became almost lost for want of being tamed.

I shall not forget this visit among these wild animals and with a gentle cattleman. This gracious raconteur of the scenic western part of the Old Dominion is a walking encyclopedia of buffalo knowledge. I enjoy talking with people about things that interest them.

I have yet to meet the man who could not teach me something I did not know. Guess that's why I profit so much from the fine enjoyment of listening.

It's Time To Fly A Kite

Sometimes I yearn to leap across an uncrossable gulf, the span that separates now from what once was. Times then were simple. Problems and worries did not seem nearly as difficult. Springtime brought baseball and marbles. And the winds of March were for flying kites.

I've wondered who invented the kite. Some say it was the Greek scientist Archytas of Tarentum in 400 B.C. But a little reading in Asian history tells us that the Koreans, Chinese, Japanese and Malayans have been flying this simple apparatus from time immemorial. Flying a kite surely has been overlooked in recounting the giant strides made by man. For hands that first carved crude tools and weapons for survival turned to creating a novelty from a dream to be used for the fantasy of the imagination. The idea probably originated while watching the soaring of a hawk. At least there is an association in the name that became its identity.

If I can but find one day to be free from all that is pressed upon me, I shall teach my grandson the science of the kite. Store-bought rigs seem to be artificial imitations. A boy needs to create that which he flies. And this experience of learning will blend a touch of the science of aerodynamics, aeronautics and architectonics. All these were what boys specialized in on the hill where I lived.

We carefully selected three dried stalks of weeds in equal size and length and tied them together at a center point. A string was tightly strung to the outward tips of the weeds to form the design of this artful aerodyne. Then, old newspapers were carefully pasted to the frame. The harness, measured by the width of the kite, had to be precisely attached to the center and the forward ends. To this was tied the cord that would allow us to control the apparatus in flight. A tail was added to the bottom of the frame to give balance. This long appendage was made up of scraps from Aunt Effie's quilting box. That good soul of long ago probably helped build more kites, and, later, wrote more letters to nephews away at war than any woman I know. Every boy needs a maiden aunt who saves strings and stuff to share with kids who need to play.

I shall make the time to fly a kite. For the things I leave undone shall soon pass and not be counted. But a day invested in teaching a small boy a simple pleasure from the past may someday be recalled.

And if he does remember, whenever it is, and wherever I am, I shall be glad that among my hectic days on earth my grandson and I knew the joy of flying a kite.

Rocking Chairs & Little Things

Old-fashioned rocking chairs with cane bottoms give illusions of peace and tranquility. Their presence on any porch is an invitation to Southern hospitality and gentle living. Rockers at the hearth bring to mind familiar faces and generate wishes for places once known and doors long closed.

These relics of other days silently speak of placid times when life was not hurried and there was ample time to visit and relax. They bring to remembrance Grandma's soft lap, Uncle's many stories, and friendly neighbors who came at dusk to sit until bedtime. Those days seem now entirely of another era. But recollections of those little things are refreshingly revived at the mere mention of a rocker on a hot summer's day.

Papa's rocker was reserved and hallowed. No child, or for that matter nobody in his right mind-would have dared sit in Papa's chair. From this seat he ruled as supremely over all he owned as did John the Third of England in the royal palace. In the name of progress two old resorts in recent years were replaced by plush motels. But to my way of seeing things, the charms of both Mammoth Cave and Lake Junaluska were destroyed when they demolished the wide and rambling veranda once lined with friendly and genial rocking chairs.

This spring I bought a rocker for our side porch. For too many years I've planned to enjoy a summer and capture as many hours that time could afford, to do nothing but sit and rock and watch birds and trees, and inhale sweet scents of boxwoods and fallen apples.

But summer has come and is madly rushing on. And my chair is empty and unused and alone. And someday, somewhere, I'll look back with remorse that I didn't take time for these little things. For some things can be lost that can never be recovered.

Veteran's Day

It is difficult for one who never heard the sound of a bugle and the rattle of a distant drum to understand the kinship of those who have served and now wear the honorable title of veteran. Strong ties form a mutual loyalty among those who have sacrificed in the wars.

Young soldiers of every campaign complain about the food, and the sergeant, and the captain. Sons react to the regimentation and hardship as did their fathers before them. There is no difference. Soldiers are the same in every age. Yet, those who survived the hell of battle somehow mellow with years to remember they met that challenge with honor. And this gives a pride which cannot be described or explained. Nevertheless, it remains a deep and lasting substance in the soul of every old soldier.

The sound of martial music on Veteran's Day brings a retrospection of the old corps...to hear once more the sound of the bugle and the rattle of a distant drum. And the veteran will recall some scenes with silence, for these cannot be spoken... always hidden within the breast...the stenciled name on a white cross among the thousands of graves at St. Mere Eglise, a friend lost in battle who could not be given a burial or even a common grave.

These thoughts and a thousand more are with the veteran on Veteran's Day. He does not glorify the tactics of war. He is not immune to the sufferings of humanity. The veteran knows that he was called to serve in the defense of all he loves. And for this he gave his best.

It really does not matter so much to him that others may not understand. For this is Veteran's Day. The grand colors soon will pass in review. And that pride of a high and noble cause will swell once more within his soul...and he will hear from afar the sound of a bugle and the rattle of a distant drum.

Exciting Things

I remember the excitement of crossing the North Atlantic. The wind and ice penetrated to the bone. But our boat was loaded with soldiers who did not mind. It had been a long time since we had seen home.

All hopes were aimed at making it in time for Christmas. Deep in the crowded compartments of the ship we sang "Jingle Bells" and "Silent Night" and talked about all the holiday things we could remember.

Eleven deliberate days on those stormy waves seemed like endless ages. Then, one night a sailor announced that if we could endure the cold deck, the lights of New York would soon be visible. I braved the wind and ice, and shall not soon forget that experience. Never has a light been more welcomed... never a moment more exhilarating. I'm not much at crying. Soldiers never cry. But I think I almost did that night.

I recapture that tender moment every now and then as I travel the crowded way of life. This helps me to separate the little things from the big things...the trivial from the significant... and when to remain calm and the times to leap for joy. And the most exciting thing I know is that moment on a long road when you turn around and head for home!

Paths In The Brier Patch

One of the grandest welcomes I know about is to be greeted at the dining table with a piping hot blackberry cobbler, right out of the oven, and so hot you sit awhile and whistle until it's cooled off enough to eat.

Blackberry pies, like most of the best things in life, are not easy to come by. A man has to be prepared for a certain amount of punishment and a little suffering when he heads for the brier patch of sharp thorns that guard the juicy berries. But the cobbler on the supper table is worth all the inconveniences and the heat of a summer's sun.

This pulpy fruit was a delicacy among our ancient Celtic and Anglo-Saxon ancestors. In fact, it is considered by historians to be among the very earliest of edible fruits in the north temperate zones of the old and new worlds. There is evidence that the Ice Age brought together two widely different berry groups of the northern and southern climate zones.

This prehistoric hybridization of probably not more than twenty original species gave the northern climates of the earth literally thousands of varieties of these delicious berries. The biggest miracle of this quirk of nature's hybrid meddling was that the seeds were able to reproduce themselves. According to horticulturists there are now thousands of hybrids and segregates of various types of blackberries in North America alone.

The variety found in our hills of the Southeastern part of the United States is the Eastern Group. Consisting of both the erect and trailing stems, this group ranges from Southern Florida to Canada and west to the Great Plains.

Blackberries were plentiful on our place this year. Our grandchildren took upon themselves the daily task of inspecting to see when the berries were right and ready for picking. On those evenings selected for harvesting they would be at the house waiting in overalls with buckets in hand for this specialized work.

Grandpa's job was to lead the way, and to make neat paths through the impenetrable forest of fortified briers for smaller pickers to follow. We enjoyed the finite strategy and maneuvering it required to reach the unreachable clusters that always seemed to be just beyond where a person can go.

I shall wish to remember this year's berry picking season with so abundant a crop. Already, though the berries are now gone, I find myself appraising the paths that conquered the un-conquerable thickets to reach the fruits that whetted our appetites while thinking ahead about Grand-mother's cobbler pie.

I would wish, too, that this little boy and girl remember these fun paths in the brier patch. I hope they'll recall that the best in life will be worth all the effort and challenge and hard work it takes to reach a noble goal.

Little George, The Mountain, & Me

This mountain is not too easy to find unless you know where it is. And it's almost hidden among the ranges of the Blue Ridge near Waynesboro, Virginia. My Daddy talks often of staying at this lodge. The thin and crisp air at these altitudes does something wonderful for sleep. But the best part is the way it whets an appetite at dawn before the thick mist of hovering clouds has time to melt away.

I was pleased the way little George took to these sharp and winding curves and climbed the steepest grades. Mister Ollie always said the best way to ignite the wood and to lay a good burning flame is to name the fire before you light it. Some folks talk to house plants and claim it helps them grow. Maybe it helps us to give a personal touch to an impersonal thing. I don't know.

Anyhow, I've always named my cars. That's one reason I keep them so long...and when, finally they have to be traded in, it is much like losing a true and valued friend.

Little George is new, a small compact, with only four cylinders; no artificial air conditioning, and no radio to disturb or distract from the thoughts while being alone with yourself. I've read that big cars are status symbols. I wouldn't know much about that. The best prestige among the folk I like are honesty, sincerity, and the noble ability to just be themselves with no airs or pretension.

Sitting here alone tonight among the timbers that grow in lofty places I feel the assurance of time and space and eternity. Everything has its place in the order of things. It's hard to understand this in crowded cities, and among heart-breaking problems we face as we live our life. Man does not grow too old to suffer, but he can know that someday, somewhere, somehow it will all fit together in a grand and masterful plan.

The climb was long and hard and weary from the valley to these heights. There was stress and strain on the limited power of four little cylinders. But how gratifying to be here...little George...the mountain...and me.

The Cedar

Today I planted a cedar. It was not the first, and I hope not the last. It may well be that I have defied the old superstition: "He who plants a cedar will die before it grows to shade his grave."

I once read there are 865 species of trees native to the continental United States, if the few imports that have become naturalized are counted. Have seen only a fraction of these. But of the few I know and appreciate, the cedar is by far my favorite.

Cedars are somehow associated with ancient things. In stately grace they dominate old homesteads to join in harmony the earth and building and sky. Their ageless appearance suggests they do outlive those who build the home and plant the trees.

The evergreen character of the cedar is a promising reminder of the eternal order of the universe. Its deep green foliage in pliant sprays enhances the darkest days of winter as well as the warmest days of spring.

The cedar is a Holy Land and Bible tree. The earliest specifications for builders called for its sturdy and enduring timbers. Characters of men and nations were compared to its pyramidal contour and its broad trunk. The ancient psalmist declared:

> The trees of the Lord are full of sap;
> the cedars of Lebanon which he hath planted.

An ancient sign hangs at the entrance to a park in Portugal. If it were possible, these thoughts would guard my small forest when others come into possession of these trees I love.

> Ye who would pass by and raise your hand against me, harken ere you harm me. I am the heat of your hearth on the cold winter nights; the friendly shade screening you from the summer sun. I am the beam that holds your house, the board of your table, the bed on which you lie, and the timber that builds your boat. I am the handle of your hoe, the door of your homestead, the wood of your cradle, and the shell of your coffin. I am the gift of God and friend of man.

The Knowledge Of May

We don't celebrate with festivities the beginning of May as in some parts of the world. But I recall the enthusiasm of long ago when we were allowed, at last, to shed shoes and long underwear on that eventful occasion. Then, the more hearty of our lot would cautiously plunge into the cold spring-fed hole behind the mill.

I frequently take trips into the woods. And like to drive along back roads. Here are handiworks of the Omnipotent. Things are not too small or insignificant to escape the Master's deliberate detail of design and arrangement. I stand amazed before the sculpture of the mighty tree trunk, and in admiration before the fine art in each petal of the trillium and seven-bark. The forests of the earth are cathedrals of the world. Man can never duplicate their architecture. And wonderful it is that no two are exactly alike.

My grand moment of May is the solitude found in silent journeys that lead to deep woods where trees stand alone-far from the echoes of man. That which I covet most is a time to be quiet...and a time to think...and a time to listen.

May portrays the splendor of earth and nature. Trees are pure viridian, roses are blooming, and garden plants are maturing. All things are new and fresh, and even the sky has calmed from the turbulent spring.

I think I should love to live to fully understand all the knowledge that comes to me in May. But life is too swift...and May is much too brief.

Daddies At Graduation

I sat high in the bleachers tonight and watched my oldest daughter receive her college degree with honor. The evening before, I saw this same young lady stand with the elite corps of nurses and receive the coveted pin of a profession that is honored and respected around the world.

It's not easy to put into words the satisfaction and gratitude and pride a Daddy feels at graduation time. For this goal, you see, was set for this little girl long before that exciting first day when with laughing eyes she entered school and captured the entire first grade with her special kind of effervescence.

There were so many memories tonight as I looked at her tiny figure in the dignified academic gown. I felt a similar excitement when I waited in a faraway army camp to see my little two-year-old alight from a passenger train and run across the platform into my life again. I recall with apprehension the time I lost her in a big city...terror and despair...and, then, the ultimate relief when I dis-covered that our independent toddler had somehow made her way safely to the family car. I'll never forget the way she hugged me when she discovered her own horse hidden in the stable on her birthday...and the time her Daddy agreed that she had grown up when, arriving home from an Easter cantata, she delivered a foal at the far side of our pasture... while still wearing her formal gown and white high heels.

Everybody knows that a time comes in the life of young ladies when Daddies fade silently into the background. But nobody ever told me that a Daddy's world would be filled with so much music at life's major milestones... like graduation time.

Fahrenheit And Celsius

Weather watching, especially in January and February, has been practiced as long as I can remember. I've known some highly accurate forecasters over the years. And noted, too, a kind of psychological pride as to whose thermometer showed the lowest readings on the coldest morning.

In this part of our world a zero weather report is a serious matter. This, of course, is based upon our instrumentation developed by a German born in 1685. Gabriel Daniel Fahrenheit was a seller of weather gauges, and lived most of his life in England and Holland. He used mercury instead of alcohol in his thermometer; his freezing point registered at 32 degrees, and boiling point at 212 degrees.

We are hearing a new word in temperatures. Every time degrees in Fahrenheit are given, the announcer is required to slip in another reading known as Celsius. Now, believe me, this is going to be mighty important in a few years. Because, by the time we wonder how it all came about, Fahrenheit will become a part of our dead language, and Celsius will be all we get. We are now in the official "phase-in" part of one of the most dramatic changes in weather-reporting history.

Anders Celsius died at the age of 43, a few years before George Washington was born. He invented his thermometer several years after the English world had accepted Fahrenheit. Young Anders Celsius was something of a genius in his day. No one knows just why he was tinkering around with temperatures, in that he was Professor of Astronomy at the University of Uppsala in Sweden. His device had a more sensible arrangement, with a freezing line at zero and a boiling point at 100.

Now, any school boy knows that to change Fahrenheit to centigrade, all you do is subtract 32 from the Fahrenheit and multiply by five over nine.

But we who have lived under the old Fahrenheit, 32 degrees for freezing and 212 degrees for boiling, will have to do a lot more than subtract, multiply, and divide. We'll need to adjust our whole way of thinking. And that will be the hardest part of all.

This Is Life

One of the delights of life is to be in the presence of a little child. They have a simple philosophy, a contagious faith, and a cheerful wisdom. My six-year-old grandson is my sidekick for tractor work. Together we tackle chores that involve a lot of drudgery and sometimes difficult tasks. He likes riding in the trailer with feet dangling over the side. And calls this the fun part; but never fails to do more than a fair share of the hard kind.

Sometimes we overdo things, and grow tired and exhausted. But he never seems to be any less energetic than that hour we first began. Today, though, was different. Carter mashed his hand. I tried to comfort, and offered my sympathy and concern. But that little boy measured pretty tall in my estimation when he held back the tears, looked up at me, and said, "Don't worry, Granddaddy, this is life, you know."

I've since thought these hours about his swollen hand, and how I wish it had been me instead of him, and the insight of his youthful words. He called to my mind certain realities we sometimes are prone to forget. Life affords no shelters to protect us from the unpleasant. We are guaranteed no day free from trouble. There is no escape from our portion of sorrow. A lot of people are in pain; I find them everywhere I go.

I know, too, that grandfathers would, if they could, protect little ones from even the smallest obstacle or the slightest pain. But boys do not become men with fiber and strength until they face the fear, share the sorrow, and endure the pain. For this is life, you know.

Sign Of Progress

Last night a squirrel barked in the oak behind our house. It was a good sign that another season is changing. Days are growing shorter, and logs soon will be kindled in the fireplace.

Sounds of the squirrel brought back the reminiscence of a nostalgic farm in southern Tennessee. We called it "the old home-place." There was a barn so big we could hide for hours in a corner and not be found. A springhouse seemed to grow from old rocks. It was always cool, damp, and covered with slippery moss. The hill on the other side of the branch concealed a secret cave, and offered chestnuts, scaly barks,

and fox squirrels in the fall. As a boy I wondered if maybe Heaven would be somewhat similar to this wonderful place.

I wish now I could tear away the recollections of my last visit. This trip I try so hard to forget. Bulldozers had invaded my green and ageless paradise to leave scars and gashes where once stood ancient hills and trees. The brook that used to wind casually through bending branches and vines and ferns had been demolished to leave only the ugliness of a straight ditch and piles of bare earth.

I would trade a thousand dreams to forget that I went back again. Better to have wondered and never known. Better to have remembered as it once had been. Better to not have seen a senseless sign of progress.

But man and machines can only destroy things seen-never those things we hold within ourselves as treasured memories.

Chocolate-Covered Cookies

I'm no good at shopping for groceries, staples and such. Never know where things are; cannot determine just what and how much is needed; and have no concept of bargain prices. But I do enjoy getting a basket and wandering from aisle to aisle, looking mostly, and buying sparingly; and even then, purchasing only the delicacies that please my fancy.

I hesitated awhile ago at the sweets section, and reached for a box of cookies that had fallen from its place on the stack. These chocolate-covered graham cracker cookies looked like they did when they tempted a small boy a long time ago. Holding the cookie box, I detected the faint fragrance of old times, and my mind drifted back to Grandpa's general store. Grandpa kept these cookies in large bins covered with a hinged glass top to be dispensed by hand as we counted out our pennies. What a difference from all the modern prepackaging we are accustomed to everywhere we go!

Today, nothing is left of even the building. There's not a sign on the earth to indicate where Grandpa's store once stood. It was a clean white structure and most surely would be lost in a corner of a twentieth-century supermarket. That old store seemed always to have a fresh coffee-bean smell, mixed with aromas of stalk-ripened bananas, salt pork, stacks of Happy Cow Feed, flavors of peppermint and horehound candies, as well as dozens of other things.

People would often eat lunch in stores back then. There were the cracker barrel and the hoop of sharp cheese.

Anyone could add variety by opening a can of beans or sardines or a jar of peanut butter.

I clerked and was delivery boy and did a lot of other chores. My uncles soon taught me the rudiments of driving Grandpa's Model A truck while standing on the wooden floor; young legs hauling groceries just could not reach the foot pedals while sitting on the seat.

I have a feeling that many things in my life would have gone in other directions had it not been for the powerful influence I got from Grandpa while working in his store. This man who looked so important in his long white apron taught me a whole lot about life's lasting priorities. And I've been trying ever since to make as good a showing as possible for all the high hopes that wonderful man held for me. With a Grandpa like him a fellow really has to try.

Replacing the magic box of chocolate-covered cookies, I left the complex food store realizing once again that yesterdays can live forever because they are so much a part of what we are now.

A Tribute To Mattie

I sat around a coffee table at a well-known Memphis hotel with some old-timers today. One was a banker, and the other a retired real estate developer. Each had interesting stories of Memphis and her people. They told of how things are today and the way they used to be.

The banker was anxious to show us a mausoleum in a modern cemetery that had all the appearances of an impregnable fortress. This vast domain for the dead had spaces niched in the walls for three thousand departed souls. He said it had already cost more than a million and a half, and is not yet completed. Now, I'm impressed, but cannot help thinking how much good all that money could do for the living.

We drove from the modern cemetery to an old and well cared for one at the other side of town. Not many living come here today, but a whole lot of Memphis lies buried within its silent walls. There is an interesting statue of a lady near the main gate. Her name, Mattie Stevenson, is carved on the stone.

Mattie was a notorious owner of a house of ill repute in the red-light district, more than a hundred years ago. Society avoided the likes of this woman. But the terrible scourge of Yellow Fever in 1878-79 changed her status. Mattie and her ladies of the evening became angels of mercy. Her infamous house became a hospital. Mattie caught the fever and gave her life while caring for the sick and dying. A grateful city erected this lasting tribute to a lovely Mary Magdalene.

Back at the hotel we drank more coffee and told more tales, and I couldn't keep my eyes from the words on a sign near the cash register. It said, "You are never going to get anywhere if you think you are already there." I copied its message in my journal, for someday I'm going to think about what it means.

Calendars And Gardens

March is here at last! Been looking forward to its arrival since January. March 25th was originally New year's Day in old England and the early American colonies. In fact, George Washington was twenty years old when the calendar was changed. The Romans developed the Julian calendar in 46 B.C. It contained a serious error, and Pope Gregory XII made the correction in 1582. One hundred and seventy years later our English forebears finally accepted the Gregorian calendar, and New year's Day was changed to January 1.

Our Anglo-Saxon ancestors were deep rooted in the ways of nature. It took long years for the works of Julius Caesar and Pope Gregory to affect their calendar.

The Department of Agriculture predicts there will be thirty-two million home gardens planted this spring. That's refreshing news! It will help inflated food prices and provide healthful and low-cost recreation. And I've always believed that a garden contains more therapeutic healing for mind and soul than a sophisticated medical clinic. There is no better way to unwind from cares and woes than by tilling the earth and watching tender plants grow.

Catching The Boat

The other evening my grandson followed me to my upstairs study. He likes to go there almost as much as I enjoy his presence. I often think it's because of the old guns, swords, and other relics standing about the room, although his mother strongly objects to his association with anything that resembles a weapon or a battle.

He turned his attention this time to two lovely portraits on the wall. "Who are they?" he asked. I explained that one is my mother and the other is my grandmother. With a spark of anticipation he said, "Let's go see them." I tried to explain the best I could that they are far away and we cannot go there.

He studied my words and explained to me, "Yes, we can, Grand-daddy. All we need to do is to catch the boat." At first, I dismissed this as a childish whim. Yet, in the passing of these days his words have become indelible in my mind. What a great message of hope and truth. For indeed we can go there. And it really is as simple as catching the boat.

Books And Folk

There was a book in our boyhood home with an adventurous title, *The Book of Wonders*. This volume, and the old Family Bible on top of Pa's chifforobe, kindled a spark within a young boy. It became a burning flame of inquiry and subsequent enchantment with the printed word. It flared over the years into a hunger and thirst for knowledge that will never be fulfilled.

Books are as much a part of our home now as the paper on the walls. They are friends. Each addition is like finding a new acquaintance. Older collections become more mellow with age.

I've been thinking how some books in many ways are like most people. Usually we are tempted to judge by outside appearance. Yet, when we dig deeper, some of the best in a book and the rarest and most beautiful qualities in people are discovered from what seems at first to be the ordinary.

To write a book has long been a dream. Now it seems far beyond probabilities. Days and years have come and gone too quickly. However, if it were possible, the subject would surely be about people. But not about the rich or powerful or renowned... they have their biographers. My composition would sing the unsung tales of those who live in villages and in the country and work on the farms and in the factories and shops. Inspirational and challenging stories are found among those who live in simple ways, and work by the sweat of the brow. Wisdom and reason can be learned from a trusting faith of those who fight and lose and try again another day.

It has been said that the woman or man whose biography is not worth writing has not yet been born. To believe in the Creator and in man is to know that no birth is accidental or without consequence. I believe that in every newborn baby there are limitless possibilities. And in the old and bent and age-worn can be found a wealth of practical philosophy that the best-endowed libraries can never provide. And I believe that, as every book has some meaning to give, every man has a purpose to live.

FLORENCE

Historian Bill McDonald dies

By Michelle Rupe Eubanks
Staff Writer

William "Bill" McDonald, Florence historian, Korean War veteran, United Methodist preacher and longtime TimesDaily columnist, died Sunday in Florence at Mitchell-Hollingsworth Nursing and Rehabilitation Center of complications related to Parkinson's Disease.

He was 82.

McDonald's biography could have stopped and started with his military career, 38 years that began when he became one of the first members to graduate from the ROTC program at the University of North Alabama. Of course, mention would have to be made of the years he spent as a United Methodist minister as well as work he did as chief of the budget staff for the Tennessee Valley National Fertilizer Development Center.

To do that, however, would be to omit his passion and the one thing he's perhaps most well-known for: Shoals history.

Jim Hannon/File

William McDonald reflects during Memorial Day services at Veterans Park on May 31, 2004.

"Once a week, on Wednesdays, he would come to the library, and, whenever he was there, he would sit at this round table, and no less than eight to 10 to 12 people would sit there with him, and whatever he wanted to talk about, they would talk about," said Nancy Sanford, director of the Florence-Lauderdale Public Library. "In our minds at the library, he's a hero for the community in that he dedicated his life to saving and retelling and documenting the history and stories of this community."

McDonald's love of local history began as a child. Born in Florence, he would sit at his grandmother's feet, listening to her recount the stories of what life was like in the area in the 1800s and at the turn of the century.

It wasn't long before McDonald became the keeper of those stories, telling them to others. In addition to amassing the spoken accounts of Colbert and Lauderdale counties, often through first-person interviews and extensive research, McDonald also acquired countless letters, photos and other historical documents that, when combined, create a tangible history of the Shoals.

Throughout his lifetime, McDonald became the authority on the Sweetwater area of Florence, including the mill villages that sprang up there, UNA's early years

in Colbert County on the LaGrange Mountain and its subsequent move to Lauderdale County as well as the history of the United Methodist Church in the Shoals.

From 1968 until 1989, he served as the chairman of the Florence Historical Board, and, in 1989, he was appointed Florence City Historian. In 1979, he published the first of 15 books he would write. "Paths in the Briar Patch" was McDonald's memoir of growing up in the Shoals. His last book, "Civil War Tales of the Tennessee Valley," was published in 2003.

Angela Broyles, co-founder of Bluewater Publications, has made it among her goals to see each of McDonald's books back into print for a new, younger audience, one less familiar with the good old days.

"He has some of the most well-documented history of the area, and it shouldn't disappear," she said.

It was "Paths in the Briar Patch" that brought McDonald into contact with another local historian, Harry Wallace, of Florence.

"I guess it was sometime in the 1970s because I was teaching at Central High School at the time, and I heard he was doing a book-signing, and I went to go meet him. I pretty much knew his family all my life," Wallace said.

"He found out I was a history teacher, and he took me under his wing, and helped me. He was so good at what he did that people who wouldn't normally open up would open up to him. But he knew enough about what he had and the value of it, and he dedicated most of it to UNA.

"That's one of the great gifts he leaves. I'm just sorry for the kids who won't get to hear him tell his stories," he said.

The vacancy he leaves as city historian will also be difficult to fill, Florence Mayor Bobby Irons said.

"He did a wonderful job and spoiled us with the knowledge he had available," Irons said.

"He did such a good job it would be a shame not to continue this because he's proven how important that position is to the city," he added.

To Lee Freeman, in the local history and genealogy department at the Florence library, there are no feet big enough to fill those shoes.

"I would come in on Wednesdays and sit at the round table and listen to him," Freeman said. "Anytime someone came in asking for help, he would help them and encourage them. He was never territorial. If he ever made a mistake, which was rare, he would admit it. But there wasn't a whole lot he got wrong."

McDonald was married to Dorothy Carter McDonald, an artist and retired teacher in the Florence City School System. They have two daughters, Dr. Nancy Carter McDonald and Suzannah Lee McDonald.

Staff Writer Trevor Stokes contributed to this report. Michelle Rupe Eubanks can be reached at 740-5745 or michelle.eubanks@Times-Daily.com.

Published by

Bluewater Publications is a multi-faceted publishing company capable of meeting all of your reading and publishing needs. Our two-fold aim is to:

1) Provide the market with educationally enlightening and inspiring research and reading materials and to
2) Make the opportunity of being published available to any author and or researcher who so desires to become published.

We are passionate about preserving history; whether it is through the re-publishing of an out-of-print classic or by publishing the research of historians and genealogists, Bluewater Publications is the publisher you need.

To learn more about the Dr. William Lindsey McDonald or for information about how you can be published through Bluewater Publications, please visit:

www.BluewaterPublications.com

Confidently Preserving Our Past,
Angela Broyles and Crystal Broyles
Bluewater Publications.com
Formerly Known as Heart of Dixie Publishing

Printed in the United States
91061LV00003B/197-246/A

9 781934 610060